JOHN DE COURCY
PRINCE OF ULSTER

JOHN DE COURCY
PRINCE OF ULSTER

STEVE FLANDERS

COLOURPOINT

Published 2015 by Colourpoint Books
an imprint of Colourpoint Creative Ltd
Colourpoint House, Jubilee Business Park
21 Jubilee Road, Newtownards, BT23 4YH
Tel: 028 9182 6339
Fax: 028 9182 1900
E-mail: info@colourpoint.co.uk
Web: www.colourpoint.co.uk

First Edition
First Impression

Designed by April Sky Design, Newtownards
Tel: 028 9182 7195
Web: www.aprilsky.co.uk

Printed by W&G Baird Ltd, Antrim

ISBN 978-1-78073-069-1

Front cover: Carrickfergus Castle, centre of John de Courcy's kingdom. *(Sam Knox)*
Opening image: Downpatrick seen from Inch Abbey. *(Steve Flanders)*
Closing image: Carrickfergus Castle at night. *(Sam Knox)*

About the author:
Steve Flanders studied the Courcy family for his doctoral thesis at Queen's University Belfast. He lectures and tutors on a wide range of topics, especially the medieval period.

Contents

Thanks

I should like to thank Carrickfergus Borough Council and the Northern Ireland Environment Agency, without whose support this book would not have been possible. Thanks also to Ian Eagleson and John O'Keefe and their staffs for all their help, and especially Sam Knox for the generous use of his photographs of Carrickfergus Castle.

Generously supported by:

Dawn, early February 1177. The Hill of Down, today's Cathedral Hill, stands out from the mist which flows across the countryside; the mist that makes it difficult to distinguish the surrounding flooded tidal marshes from what will become the town of Downpatrick. As the sun rises higher, it reveals a mass of armed men approaching the fords across the Quoile river to the north. Thousands strong and confident, they are led by their king, keen to recapture his hill fort. Up on the hillside a few hundred men await their attack. Dismounted knights and men-at-arms, protected by chain mail, holding swords and spears, and backed up by archers and lightly-armed allies, survey the approaching army, confident of victory. Unlike the oncoming native Irish, the defenders are mostly Normans – fierce warriors, trained to fight from birth, and conquerors of England, Sicily and Jerusalem. And they have another advantage. Standing tall amongst them, fair-haired, experienced, courageous and full of confidence, is the aristocrat who will lead them to victory and win for himself a kingdom. He is John de Courcy, and he will this day become Prince of Ulster.

John de Courcy was born in the middle of the twelfth century, in about 1150, at the manor of Middleton Cheney in Northamptonshire. His father, Jordan, was lord of the manor. There do not appear to have been any previous children born to Jordan and his wife (her name has not survived in the records). Stillborns, infant deaths and daughters were not recorded and even the birth date of John is conjectural. It's likely that Jordan de Courcy married a year or so before John's arrival although, of course, he and his younger brother – named Jordan after his father – may have been born some years after the marriage. Their father, like all Anglo-Norman aristocrats, would only have married when he had secured sufficient land and wealth to satisfy his future wife's family that he had the ability to support his bride and any children they might have. Ownership of sufficient land also demonstrated that Jordan's social status matched or exceeded that of his bride's family. To marry, he needed to hold land or have good prospects of doing so. Jordan did not marry before he became lord of Middleton Cheney in Northamptonshire.

Middleton Cheney, or rather Middleton Courcy as it would have been known at the time, was a moderately-sized manor centred on a village together with several hamlets and land suitable for different types of agriculture, both arable and pastoral. Like most medieval manors it was largely self-sufficient, producing all the food and materials that the lord of the manor, his family, sub-tenants and peasants needed to survive. Jordan sub-divided Middleton not only into the different land types but also amongst sub-tenants. Some of these would have been fairly well-to-do farmers whilst others were little more than agricultural labourers, living in small cottages with a garden for growing vegetables and access to a modest share of any common land. These tenants used surplus food, raw materials such as animal hides, and their own labour to pay the lord in return for the use of the land. Good-quality land produced various crops, animals were reared in pastures, meadows were cut to provide winter hay, and bogs were cut for turf fuel. Poorer quality high ground was ideal for sheep and goats, whilst woodland provided everything from foraging for pigs to construction material.

Jordan de Courcy was given the lordship of the manor of Middleton Cheney by his older brother William who had inherited their father's much larger lordship – the honour of Stogursey. This Courcy lordship in England comprised manors scattered across the country, although mainly concentrated in Somerset, Devon and Yorkshire.

In granting Jordan the manor of Middleton, William was fulfilling his duty of providing for his siblings and other family members. However, the grant was not absolute. Like all medieval transfers it contained an element of quid pro quo.

Nominally, the king of England owned all the land. All the lords, the Church and others were his tenants – known as tenants-in-chief. These then tenanted some of their lands to men lower down the social scale, such as younger brothers, who became lords of manors like Middleton Cheney. William de Courcy was one of these tenants-in-chief and his brother Jordan one of these lesser men. Lesser he may have been but, like all such men holding only one or two modest manors, he played a vital role in twelfth-century society.

Jordan owed William fealty, that is fidelity and loyalty. He was William's 'man'. When required, Jordan would turn out as a mounted knight to support his lord. This is why from an early age all aristocratic boys were trained to fight, unless they were destined for a career in the Church. Aristocratic girls were trained by their mothers in the skills necessary to run a lord's household, that of their future husband, unless they too entered the Church.

Jordan wasn't the only trained fighting man that William could call upon. Each tenant-in-chief had a quota set by the king. When the king went to war he expected all his tenants-in-chief to muster their quota of fighting men so that, together with the king's own knights and men-at-arms, they formed the royal army, the army of England. Failure to muster your men when the king commanded meant you had committed treason which, at the very least, led to loss of land and status and, at worst, your life.

Consequently, throughout William de Courcy's lordship across England he held some of the manors himself for his own income – often the best ones – and granted the others to men who formed his personal army. The most important element of this army were the knights, usually younger sons of aristocrats who fought on horseback. Indeed, aristocratic boys were introduced to horse riding at a very young age, as soon as they could straddle a saddle, so that it became second nature to them. The more plentiful element in each lord's private army were men-at-arms, who fought on foot. They were usually tenants of the poorer manors within the lordship. Nevertheless, they still represented significant wealth compared to the peasants, not least because they could equip themselves with chain mail, like the mounted knights. Chain mail was very expensive. Every link was hand made and it took an expert blacksmith to manufacture a bespoke suit. Accurate fitting was vital as the wearer's life depended on his ability to move easily when wearing it and his confidence in its ability to protect him.

For most of the year these men lived on and administered their manors, but in the summer campaigning season between sowing and harvesting they could be called up to fight. However, by the later twelfth century a change was developing in this system of knight service. A monetary value was set on the cost of providing a mounted knight or a man-at-arms. Rather than call out each lord's tenants for campaigning, the king began to accept this monetary value from each lord according to their required quota instead of the men themselves, and used the money to hire stipendiary knights who were probably better trained for warfare and certainly had greater experience. When John de Courcy first struck out on his own independent path he became a stipendiary knight. This was a typical career path of a young aristocrat who either inherited very little wealth from his father or who was a younger son.

Although comparatively modest, Middleton Cheney provided Jordan and his family with most of what they needed throughout the year, but they would also have traded food and other things for items made by specialist craftsmen in nearby towns or brought into the district by itinerant merchants. Also, as in any farming district today, they traded cattle, sheep and other livestock with their neighbours and in the regular markets held in the district. Markets were based in towns, in fact they were the main reason for a town's existence. Towns were manors just like everywhere else in the twelfth century and they were owned by a lord or several lords. Controlling a town meant that a lord controlled its market and was able to gain a considerable income from its transactions. Jordan's manor relied on markets owned by other lords and this shows he was far from the front rank of the aristocracy. Nevertheless, although he was not wealthy when compared with other aristocrats, he enjoyed a comfortable income which was many times greater than his sub-tenants and beyond the dreams of the average labourer.

Jordan de Courcy remained lord of Middleton throughout his life and eventually passed it on to his eldest son, John, who in turn listed it as part of his dower property when he married Affreca, the daughter of the king of the Isle of Man. However, Northamptonshire was not to be the centre of John de Courcy's early life. While he was still a young child his father moved the family to Harewood in Yorkshire and it was in this part of England that John grew to adulthood and made the friends, contacts and alliances which subsequently were to serve him so well in Ulster. All aristocratic families ensured that their young sons lived, trained and relaxed with others of their social class. Friendships established at this period of their lives usually persisted throughout their adulthood. It was these friendships that formed and strengthened the complex network of personal ties which permeated England's ruling elite.

John the aristocrat

John was born into the Anglo-Norman aristocracy which had dominated the kingdom of England since its conquest in 1066, and the duchy of Normandy from the time of its establishment by Viking invaders early in the tenth century. Jordan de Courcy, his father, was one of the three sons of a certain William, the first Courcy lord of the lordship of Stogursey (ie Stoke Courcy) centred in Somerset, in south-west England. Jordan was the second of the three. John's two uncles were William, the eldest brother who succeeded their father as lord of Stogursey, and Robert, the youngest brother of whom we know little. When John's uncle, the second William de Courcy of Stogursey, inherited the lordship he provided for his younger brothers: Jordan was granted the lordship of Middleton Courcy, while Robert became his eldest brother's tenant for some houses within the important royal borough of Oxford. A borough was a town which was owned by one or more lords but which had been granted a charter giving it a certain amount of self-government. All towns were markets, and all boroughs were towns, but not all towns were boroughs.

Family connections by birth, marriage and god-parenthood were very important in John's time. Royal government administered the whole of the country, but it was far less developed or detailed than government today, and its objectives were also quite different. John and his contemporaries could not look to the government for social services such as medical care or pensions, instead they relied on their family, personal connections and contacts, many of which were established by birth. As John was his father's son he could claim whatever status that gave him. John's mother is not recorded but, as it appears his father's family was the determining influence on his life, her family may have been of lower social status than the proud Courcy clan.

The lord of each manor administered local law and justice within the territory he controlled, although this was limited to what we would consider to be civil law and minor criminal offences. Disputes between lords were settled by the king or his representative in the county, the shire reeve (sheriff), who also convened the king's court to hear major criminal cases, such as murder and rape. Thus, to some degree, justice was devolved to each tenant-in-chief and he was also expected to assist the king's sheriff in tax collection and whatever other administrative duties the king expected in the locality.

At every level of society, families provided as secure an environment as possible for the protection of their members. They sought to advance the prospects of children and ensure that family wealth stayed largely under their control. Medieval families were tight, cohesive social units consisting of several generations.

They gave status, the possibility of inheritance and daily sustenance and habitation. They also gave much more. They linked each family member with other families. Families were often already connected by previous births and marriages and, more rarely, political alliances.

This is the reason why marriage in medieval society was so significant. Marriage joined two families together, not just the bride and groom. It transferred wealth, power and influence from one family to another. The bride left the family controlled by her father or other senior male relative and became part of her husband's family. Her dowry, which amongst the aristocracy could be very substantial, was removed from the family of her birth and now became the property of her new family. To give an extreme example, when the future King Henry II married Eleanor of Aquitaine in 1152 she brought most of south-western France as her dowry. Consequently, love was not the primary reason for marriage, although it often followed, and most such alliances had been discussed and debated at length within each family, and negotiated between them before any ceremony took place.

Over-arching all of these specific personal links were those of tenancy, fealty and loyalty. To be the tenant of a lord, especially a great lord, gave the head of a family plenty of responsibilities, but also provided status, an income, additional security and someone more powerful who might help them in times of need. Medieval society was a complex web of these interconnected relationships, with families forming the primary units within which people lived. These networks permeated all sections of society, even down to peasants within their village. Although the peasants' personal wealth and influence was far more limited than society's elite, they nevertheless lived within a fabric of inter-family and inter-personal relationships. As in village life down to the nineteenth century, everyone knew everyone else, how much they owned, to whom they were related and what prospects they had. It was a society in which you knew your neighbours very well and they knew you, and everyone was suspicious of outsiders, such as travelling craftsmen or merchants.

For aristocrats, these family-based relationships were especially crucial as their wealth and resources were so much greater. Also, because only a few thousand aristocrats ruled England, they all knew a lot about most of their social equals, no matter how far away they lived, and were probably related to them, if only distantly. They regularly met together whenever the king called them to an army muster and, as they all acted to some degree on behalf of the king's government, they were in regular contact with each other and with the royal court. Just as in village peasant society, aristocrats gossiped and schemed, each aiming to get advantages over other aristocrats. Being his father's son meant that John was one of these aristocrats from birth and so automatically became a part of these convoluted personal interconnections which made up the warp and weft of twelfth-century life.

However, just as peasants could be relatively rich or poor within their village, so also the aristocracy. While it is true that, as a whole, all aristocrats were vastly rich compared with all peasants, within the aristocracy there was as much variation as in any other part of society. By comparing one aristocrat with another, it is possible to see that some were fabulously wealthy and others were relatively poor, some commanded many tenants while others were pleased to be tenants themselves, even of quite modest amounts of land. John's father was one such tenant.

Inheritance and tenancy

John's father, Jordan, was the tenant of his older brother, the second William de Courcy of Stogursey. Although primogeniture, the principle that only the eldest son should inherit the father's estates, was becoming established in the first half of the twelfth century, it was far from being written in stone and it was only in later centuries that it became an unquestioned rule of inheritance. About 50 years before William inherited the lordship of Stogursey from his father, another William

– the conqueror and king of England – had died and disposed of his holdings to his three sons in a quite different way. Convention in the late eleventh century required a father to bequeath to his eldest son those lands and other wealth which he himself had inherited from his own father. Once these were disposed of, he could then distribute in a way he thought fit any lands which he himself had acquired by marriage or conquest. King William the Conqueror gave his patrimonial lands – the duchy of Normandy – to his eldest son, Robert, but granted the lands he had conquered – the kingdom of England – to his second son, also called William. The Conqueror's third son, Henry, received cash.

About 50 years later, however, the first William de Courcy of Stogursey granted all of his lands to his own first son, named William after him, undoubtedly expecting him to make some provision for his younger brothers, but keeping the lordship itself in one piece and firmly under Courcy family control. Although the father might have been tempted to provide for all his sons by dividing up his lands, when he passed everything on to his eldest son he ensured that the integrity and strength of the lordship would be maintained. Dividing it up into three parts, even unequal parts, would have substantially reduced the financial and military strength of the lordship and consequently lowered the status of the second William de Courcy amongst his fellow aristocrats. Having established himself in England, the first William de Courcy was clearly determined that his family should maintain its status within the highly-competitive Anglo-Norman aristocracy and for that the new lord, his eldest son, needed as large a lordship as possible.

Granting tenancies to younger brothers was an ideal solution for a lord with relatively limited resources compared to more powerful aristocrats. Firstly, it demonstrated that the head of the Courcy family was looking after its other members by providing an income and modest status for younger male siblings who had inherited virtually nothing. This was the expected practice of the time. Secondly, it kept the tenancies within the family and encouraged the new lord's brothers to remain loyal to him, as younger brothers were always potential competitors. Thirdly, it slowed the increasing tendency for tenants unrelated to the lord by blood or marriage to become more independent from their lord's control.

John's youth

At his birth John was immediately an aristocrat and would be reared and trained as one. It was not only his status, it was also his future job. Aristocratic boys and youths underwent training in all the skills they would need for warfare: horse riding, use of the sword and other weapons, close-combat and, as importantly, the organisation of his personal staff of grooms and squires. Furthermore, they would have learnt the basics of command: how to lead men, how to balance the make-up of their force, what types of troops to include for each different situation, and how to organise the commissary for their needs. It is often said that every French soldier in Napoleon's army carried a field-marshal's baton in his knapsack, and for young aristocratic men in the elite warrior society of twelfth-century England that was exactly what their training attempted to achieve.

John was born to be such a warrior, but his prospects were hampered by his status. His father was a younger son and had not inherited a share of his own father's lordship. Consequently, he would have little to pass on to his sons. John was his father's eldest son and as such could have expected whatever lands Jordan might own and control, and perhaps any position he held. However, as he grew to adulthood and began to understand how his world worked, it was obvious to him that his patrimony would be very modest and do little to further his position within England's ruling elite. Moreover, John had a younger brother, named after their father, so even when he did gain whatever inheritance his father might bequeath, he would also be expected to help his own brother to some extent. John's father was rich in status but poor in resources, and it is this prospect, passed on to his eldest son, which was an important influence – probably the key influence – on John's future career and actions. Almost everything that John later achieved was driven by his inherited status, very limited resources and rather bleak prospects.

John's upbringing was dominated by training to manage a lordship, and for warfare. His personal military training took place amongst other aristocratic boys under the tutelage of experienced warriors. However, John's family's modest resources would not have supported an extensive military retinue and so he gained his training by being fostered, for a few months each time, with more wealthy families to whom the Courcys were connected. The number of families with which John could claim a personal connection and were near enough to visit dramatically increased when his father moved his family to Harewood in order to take up the administration and stewardship of the Courcy family estates in northern England. This occurred in 1153 or 1154 and meant that John grew to adulthood amongst lordships owned by families who were powerful in the region and linked by birth or marriage to the Courcys.

John trained with other young aristocrats who were members of his extended kin group, or were the sons of their tenants, and established friendships on which he could later call when he subsequently transformed Ulster into an Anglo-Norman feudal lordship. He also travelled widely across northern England, visiting

Courcy estates as well as those of related families much further afield, familiarising himself with the practicalities of administration and making additional contacts with the sons of tenants. Northern England was John's training ground and provided him with his most valuable resource in Ulster: a group of young, landless, aristocratic warriors eager to take part in conquest and secure their own land as lords themselves or as tenants of a more powerful lord.

John's ancestry

John de Courcy's successful invasion and conquest of eastern Ulster was the result of his ancestry, upbringing and training as an aristocratic knight. As part of the aristocracy of the duchy of Normandy, the Courcy family was swept up in the invasion of England in 1066 by William the Conqueror and the subsequent disputes and warfare between his three sons: Robert, William and Henry.

The earliest evidence we have of the Courcy family is in Normandy in northern France sometime in the 1030s. Robert de Courcy was the fourth son of an aristocratic warrior called Baudri the German who had been encouraged to settle in Normandy by its duke, Richard. Robert of Courcy got his surname because he was given the little settlement of Courcy as his own manor, together with some outlying villages. These are all on or near the river Dives which flows northwards through western Normandy to the duke's stronghold of Caen and then on to the Channel coast. Duke Richard also arranged a marriage for Robert. His wife, Hebrea, was the daughter of another local lord and brought more manors to Robert as her dowry.

Robert de Courcy and Hebrea had at least one child, a son whom they named after their generous duke. Richard de Courcy subsequently married another local heiress, Wandelmode, and she brought additional land to her Courcy husband. All seemed set for the Courcy family to continue as minor aristocrats farming their land deep in Calvados country and enjoying the benevolent protection of their duke.

However, in 1066 that peace was shattered. The duke – William – the grandson of the Richard who had first given the Courcy family its land, was determined to conquer a new kingdom for himself just across the sea. In late September 1066, Duke William of Normandy launched his invasion of England and subsequently defeated and killed King Harold II and his Saxon army at the Battle of Hastings on 14 October. In the years following this conquest King William the Conqueror divided England up amongst his aristocrats so that they now had land on both sides of the Channel.

There is no evidence to suggest that Richard de Courcy took part in the invasion; he was probably one of the

Norman aristocrats who remained behind in Normandy to defend the duchy while most of its fighting men were away in England. Nevertheless, he did benefit from the conquest. Sometime before 1086, when the *Domesday Book* was drawn up to list what everyone owned in England, he was given three manors in Oxfordshire: Nuneham, Sarsden and Foscot. This was quite a small reward compared to the massive estates in England which other Norman aristocrats had received, but it may have been intended to give Richard an income for acting as one of King William's justiciars. As a royal justiciar Richard's job was to act on behalf of the king and make sure that all taxes and other payments due were collected and paid into the royal treasury. Once these manors had been given to Richard they became part of the Courcy family's lordship in England and Normandy. Richard de Courcy and Wandelmode had three sons: Robert, Richard and William. They were all named after dukes of Normandy. The second son, Richard, died young leaving Robert as the heir and William with only limited prospects as the younger son.

King William the Conqueror died in 1087. Because he gave the duchy of Normandy to his eldest son, Robert, and the kingdom of England to his younger son, King William II – known as Rufus because of his ginger hair and beard – this created problems of loyalty for the Norman aristocrats. They were expected to be loyal to the king or duke wherever they owned manors. So, as they all had land in Normandy the new Duke Robert expected them to be loyal to him. However, they also had land in England so the new king expected them to be loyal only to him. It was a difficult situation for all Norman aristocrats, including Robert de Courcy. That situation got worse when the sons of William the Conqueror fell out with each other and each one tried to conquer the other. Norman aristocrats were forced to choose sides. Whichever son they chose – king of England or duke of Normandy – the other one would declare them disloyal and take away their land in his territory.

Most of Richard de Courcy's land was in Normandy so he sided – more or less – with Duke Robert. This meant that the three manors he had been given in Oxfordshire could be taken from him by King William II. During the confused fighting and political manoeuvring of the 1090s, Richard de Courcy appears not to have visited England and he consequently lost control of his Oxfordshire manors, although he was never formally declared as disloyal. In Normandy, the duchy gradually descended into chaos, as different factions fought to control territory and even the person of the ineffectual Duke Robert himself. At one point, the situation became so bad for Richard de Courcy and his family that their castle at Courcy – which still stands today – was besieged by those claiming to represent the duke. With the help of an ally, another local aristocratic family, the

Grandmesnil, he successfully fought off the attack.

The situation changed when King William II of England died in a mysterious hunting accident in the New Forest on 2 August 1100, and the youngest of the three royal brothers – Henry – dashed from Normandy to England and had himself crowned king. Meanwhile, Duke Robert had spent the previous four years on the First Crusade, where he had fought very valiantly and found himself a wealthy heiress to marry. On his return later in 1100 he felt that it was he who should have succeeded to the English throne, not his younger brother Henry. Five more years of factionalism and rivalry in Normandy did nothing to strengthen Duke Robert's rule and he was eventually overthrown by King Henry I of England at the Battle of Tinchebray in Normandy on 26 September 1106. Henry imprisoned Robert until the latter's death in 1134 and took the duchy for himself.

Two Courcy families

Richard de Courcy died sometime before 1100 during this lengthy period of unrest and was succeeded by his eldest son Robert as lord of the family's Normandy manors. As was expected at the time Robert made his younger brother, William, the tenant of some of his less valuable manors so as to provide him with a home and income. This, however, was not enough for William and his subsequent action caused the Courcy family to split into two separate sections, with one based in Normandy and the other based in England. John de Courcy was a member of the English-based family.

Before his father's death, the young William de Courcy had been with the future King Henry when the latter was living in Normandy during the 1090s. He had managed to secure a place in Henry's entourage. He next appears in the records in England soon after Henry was crowned king of England in 1100. The new King Henry immediately set about organising his own government and replaced all the favourites and officials of the previous King William II with his own men. William de Courcy was one of these men. The changeover was so noticeable that chroniclers of the time referred to these young aristocratic officials of King Henry as 'new men' who had come from nothing. They were not powerful and established landowners in their own right. This was just what King Henry wanted. They owed their position and their new wealth to him and they were ready to carry out his orders to the letter. King Henry was an astute and capable administrator, and a master at manipulating and using people to serve his ends.

He appointed William de Courcy as a royal dapifer. This meant that William became a steward acting with royal authority on the king's behalf. He helped in the administration of the king's vast collection of manors as well as ensuring that tax and other income from non-royal land was paid into the treasury. It was an important but somewhat mundane job that involved plenty of accounting and supervision. This approach to the government of England was a substantial improvement on what had gone before – at least as far as King Henry was concerned – but nobody likes paying taxes so royal stewards were not popular. The post gave William de Courcy occasional access to the king, which was something that was valued by all aristocrats, and meant that he was a small but integral part of Henry's forthright control of his kingdom.

While his younger brother, William de Courcy, was becoming a rising star in King Henry's government of England, Robert de Courcy in Normandy was lord of the family's manors in the duchy, nominally ruled by Duke Robert. Consequently, the Courcy family had split into two with each section loyal to a different lord. In England, King Henry set about rewarding William de Courcy and raising his status and authority by giving him land, the most important asset of medieval society. First he gave him some royal manors in Northamptonshire. To these he added the Oxfordshire manors of Nuneham, Sarsden and Foscot, which had been listed in *Domesday Book* as in the possession of William's father, Richard de Courcy. If the tradition of primogeniture had been followed the eldest son would have inherited all his father's land and these would have passed to William's brother, Robert de Courcy in Normandy. However, because of the ongoing dispute between England and Normandy, King Henry could regard the Oxfordshire manors as forfeited by the Courcys of Normandy and was therefore free to grant them to whoever he wished.

When William de Courcy received these Oxfordshire manors it rankled with his older brother in Normandy. It was one of the reasons for the family splitting into two parts. In the next generation the subsequent Courcy lord in Normandy would use his influence to take control of land in England owned by William de Courcy's successor and this led to John de Courcy's father – Jordan de Courcy – moving his family northwards from Middleton Cheney to Yorkshire. John de Courcy grew up in Yorkshire because of a family dispute stretching back two generations, and it was there that he learned about the fragile political situation in eastern Ulster.

King Henry of England consolidated William de Courcy's position by providing him with a wealthy widow and heiress as his wife. William married Emma de Falaise in the early 1100s. Emma's dowry included manors in north Devon and Somerset which she had inherited from her father, William de Falaise. The most important manor was called Stoke, in north Somerset, and included a castle, village and church. It was the centre of all the lands which Emma brought to her second husband and so his surname was added to its name, giving Stoke Courcy, today's Stogursey. Emma's dowry was the biggest contribution to William de Courcy's new wealth and so all of his manors – including the previous royal manors and those in Oxfordshire – now became grouped together in an honour, a collection of manors held by an aristocrat. William became lord of the honour of Stogursey.

Within a few years William de Courcy had become established as a comparatively wealthy official acting on behalf of King Henry. His loyalty was guaranteed because he owed all of his success to the king. With his new wife and new manors William established a new branch of the Courcy family in England completely independent of the senior branch in Normandy headed by his brother Robert. By 1105 King Henry had defeated and imprisoned his own brother, Duke Robert, and extended his control over Normandy so that, once again, the kingdom of England and the duchy were ruled by one man. Of course, this also meant that Robert de Courcy in Normandy had to make his peace with King Henry who, magnanimously, accepted his oath of loyalty. So, within King Henry's dominions there were now two Courcy families established and, to add to the genealogical complexity, both families usually chose the same names for their sons.

William de Courcy of Stogursey and his wife Emma had three sons: William, Jordan and Robert. While the names William and Robert were already well established in the de Courcy family, Jordan was a new introduction in this generation and was only used in the English branch of the de Courcys. It may have been a traditional name in Emma's family. As the eldest son, William succeeded his father. Jordan, the second son, only had the prospect of a subordinate tenancy. He was the father of John de Courcy.

In Normandy, Robert de Courcy had married Rohesia de Grandmesnil. This marriage was arranged in order to cement the alliance between the Courcy and Grandmesnil families. They were near neighbours in the area in Normandy south of Caen and the Grandmesnil family fought in the defence of Courcy Castle in the 1090s against Duke Robert. Robert and Rohesia had at least eight children. Unfortunately, daughters rarely appear in the records as they only achieved importance in aristocratic society when they married and transferred property from one family to another in their dowries. The sons of Robert and Rohesia were Robert, Richard, William, Ivo, Philip, Simon, Gervais and Hugh.

The royal succession

Life in Normandy and England appears to have settled down under the firm rule of King Henry but all that was to change in 1120. King Henry had married Matilda of Scotland in 1100. She was a descendant of the Saxon kings of England through her mother, Margaret, and the kings of Scotland through her father, Malcolm Canmore. They had two children: William and Matilda. In 1114 Matilda married the Holy Roman Emperor Henry V, and William was set to succeed his father as king of England.

However, disaster struck on 20 November 1120, when the White Ship carrying the 17-year-old prince and many of his teenage aristocratic friends across the Channel to England hit rocks just off the coast of Normandy and sank within sight of the port of Barfleur. William and practically all of those on board were drowned. This threw the succession to the English throne into crisis. King Henry's older brother, the imprisoned Duke Robert, had a son, William Clito, who might have a claim. Also, Henry's sister, Adela, had married the count of Blois, a territory to the south east of Normandy, and they had several sons. Henry's daughter Matilda, however, now with the title of Empress, had had no children.

Matilda's husband, the Holy Roman Emperor, died in 1125 and she was summoned back to England by her father so that he could arrange a second marriage for her that would help him secure the succession to the throne after his death. King Henry married his daughter to Geoffrey, count of Anjou in 1128. Anjou was the territory to the south of Normandy and had always been a threat to the duchy. By this marriage King Henry aimed to stop the threat to Normandy from Anjou and – hopefully – provide him with a grandson. To try and control the succession as he wished, Henry made all of his aristocrats swear on oath that they would support any future son that Matilda and Geoffrey might have. Matilda gave birth to a son in 1133 and named him Henry. A second son, Geoffrey, arrived the following year, and a third, William, in 1136. The succession appeared to be safe.

King Henry died in 1135 but the succession did not work out as he had planned. His nephew, Stephen, the son of his sister Adela of Blois, had been an important figure in Henry's court for some years. Moreover, he was an adult and an experienced aristocratic warrior and administrator while Matilda's son was less than two years old. If the Norman aristocrats remained loyal to Matilda then there would be a regency run by the Empress and her husband. To allow an Angevin to rule Norman England and Normandy was unacceptable so Stephen received plenty of support and was proclaimed king of England. However, the Empress Matilda and her husband Geoffrey of Anjou had their own faction so the stage was set for civil war. Once again the Norman aristocracy was forced to choose sides in a dispute between members of the same family, for Matilda and Stephen were cousins. Both factions began to rally support but for the first couple of years after Stephen took the throne of England the fighting only took place in southern Normandy.

By about this time Robert de Courcy of Normandy had died and been succeeded by his eldest son, also Robert. In

England, William de Courcy of Stogursey, who had been King Henry's dapifer, had also died and been succeeded by his eldest son, William. This second William de Courcy of Stogursey was the older brother of Jordan de Courcy and was therefore John de Courcy's uncle. The Courcys of England and Normandy were cousins in this generation.

The second William de Courcy of Stogursey sometimes referred to himself as a royal dapifer, but this was his way of affirming his ownership of the lands granted to his father by King Henry as there is no evidence that he ever held the post. In Normandy, his cousin, Robert de Courcy, sought appointment as a royal dapifer or seneschal to King Stephen. The situation in Normandy was increasingly unsettled by civil war and it is not clear if Robert de Courcy was ever officially granted the post. He was, however, firmly in the new king's camp and remained loyal for a couple of years until Normandy was won by the Empress Matilda. He then switched allegiance. Robert de Courcy of Normandy had married soon after he inherited from his father, although the name of his wife is not recorded. They had two sons. The first, Robert, died young, while the second, William, eventually succeeded to the Courcy manors in Normandy.

In England, the second William de Courcy of Stogursey also married soon after inheriting his father's honour. William married Avice de Rumilly and they had three sons: William, Robert and Richard. Avice was a widow and an heiress. She was a member of the wealthy Meschin family, which was closely related to the earls of Chester. Her dowry added several manors to William de Courcy's land holdings. These were scattered throughout England and one of them was probably Middleton in Northamptonshire. This was the manor that William subsequently granted to his younger brother Jordan. In time, Jordan's eldest son, John de Courcy, inherited the manor and he gave it to his wife Affreca as part of his dower in their marriage settlement. In medieval marriages the bride brought her dowry to her husband while he listed about a third of his own land as dower estates, which would support her if he died first.

Avice was not only a widow when she married the second William de Courcy of Stogursey, she was also a mother. She had a daughter, Alice, who was heir to substantial property left by her father, William Paynel. So when William de Courcy married Avice he not only received her dowry lands for himself, he also received control over his step-daughter, Alice Paynel, and her inheritance. This meant he could decide who she should marry and when. The longer he postponed Alice's marriage the longer he could control and get the benefit from her inherited manors. Also, his choice of husband for Alice could be used to his own benefit to make a new alliance or, alternatively, to aid another member of the Courcy family in England.

The Rumilly inheritance

This was not the only significant aspect of William de Courcy's marriage to Avice de Rumilly. Sometime about 1135 Avice's father and brother died in quick succession, leaving all of the Rumilly inheritance to be divided between Avice and her two sisters, Alice and Cecily. The established tradition was that the inheritance should pass to the nearest male heir, but by this time a new practice was also developing alongside primogeniture, that of parage. By this, if all male siblings had died then an inheritance could be divided between surviving sisters. However, the inheritance would not mostly go to the eldest sister, as with male heirs, but instead it would be divided more or less equally. This was because it would benefit the sisters' husbands, so there was pressure for all interested parties to get a substantial share. Moreover, as this was a relatively new idea, it needed the agreement of the king to make it legally valid.

In 1136, King Stephen travelled slowly north from London to York, partly as a way of checking on the loyalty of his aristocrats and partly dispensing justice and settling legal cases. One such case was the Rumilly inheritance and he gave his approval to the division of the manors between the three sisters. Immediately, Avice de Rumilly and her two sisters each gained considerably more land than they had had in their dowries. This meant that their husbands, including the second William de Courcy of Stogursey, suddenly found themselves owners of much more land. For William this meant that he was now lord of a substantial collection of manors in Yorkshire. It was quite a windfall.

However, there was a fly in the ointment as far as William de Courcy was concerned. In his journey northwards, King Stephen had been accompanied by Robert de Courcy of Normandy, and his younger brother Richard. They were part of the king's entourage when he settled the Rumilly inheritance. In other words, Robert de Courcy of Normandy was in the presence of the king while William de Courcy of Stogursey was far away in Somerset. Robert used his opportunity to persuade King Stephen to arrange a marriage for his younger brother Richard and he had a candidate for the bride clearly in his sights. Some time soon after King Stephen was in York, Richard de Courcy of Normandy married Alice Paynel, the step-daughter of William de Courcy of Stogursey. Richard de Courcy immediately secured Alice Paynel's own inheritance from her father, which had been under William's control as her step-father. This established him as a fairly wealthy aristocrat in Yorkshire.

In return for arranging this marriage, King Stephen got a loyal supporter established in the north of England. His action suggests that Robert de Courcy of Normandy had been made a seneschal of the duchy at the same time as the Rumilly inheritance was divided up by the king. Stephen needed all the help he could get against the Empress Matilda. There was nothing that William de Courcy of Stogursey could do to prevent this intrusion into his affairs by his Normandy cousins. William's situation then became worse. By 1137, the civil war between King Stephen and the Empress Matilda had spread to England and aristocrats were forced to choose sides. Eventually, a stalemate developed – although there was much fighting – and, broadly, the south and east of England were controlled by King Stephen while the west supported the Empress Matilda.

William de Courcy was caught between the two because he had valuable manors in the West Country and also in Oxfordshire and the south Midlands. Whoever he declared for, the other would seize his manors in their territory. Instead, he opted to keep his head down and try not to get involved. He spent the civil war in Oxford, assisted by his youngest brother Robert. He occupied one of his wall tenement houses and took part in the administration of the royal borough during these difficult times, eventually being listed as an alderman, a leader of the town's ruling corporation. Oxford was on the front line and was occupied by both King Stephen and the Empress Matilda at different times. It put William in the middle of the action without committing himself to either side and also allowed him to keep a close eye on his own manors of Nuneham, a short way down the river Thames, south of the borough, and Sarsden, his valuable estate in the Cotswolds to the west. At the same time he made his brother Jordan tenant of Middleton Cheney in Northamptonshire so that he could oversee the scattering of Courcy manors in the south Midlands.

This meant that William de Courcy of Stogursey had no chance of personally supervising his wife's new inheritance in Yorkshire. Consequently, Richard de Courcy, now established in the county, seized his cousin's estates for himself, although no doubt he responded to any query as to his right to do so by saying he was merely looking after them on William's behalf during these difficult times. Moreover, as a loyal supporter of King Stephen, he had the backing of royal authority. For the Courcy family of Normandy this was payback with a vengeance. They might have lost their Oxfordshire manors a generation earlier but they now controlled much more extensive lands in Yorkshire which they had prised out of the hands of their cousin in England.

The Scottish connection

To add to this period of chaos and upheaval, King David of Scotland decided to exploit the situation to see what he could gain. He invaded the north of England, supposedly to support the Empress Matilda. His army made its way down the eastern side of the Pennines and met an English army raised by local Yorkshire lords at Cowton Moor, Northallerton on 22 August 1138. The encounter is known as the Battle of the Standard because the Normans had a mast mounted on a cart in the middle of their camp which contained the consecrated host and from which flew various religious banners. The Scots' attack was stopped and turned back but the Normans were not strong enough to pursue and destroy them. Instead a truce was established and for the next six years the Scots occupied most of northern England and had their southern capital at Carlisle. Richard de Courcy was one of the leaders of the Norman lords who fought at the Battle of the Standard. He fought on behalf of King Stephen, justifying his loyalty and repaying the king's approval of his marriage to Alice Paynel.

Earlier, a section of the Scots' army had broken away from the main body and crossed over the Pennines to the west. This force was led by William fitz Duncan, a relative of King David of Scotland. He was met by a force led by the Lacy family at their town of Clitheroe. The battle took place on 10 June and the Lacy forces were defeated. William fitz Duncan immediately marched on Skipton Castle which he easily captured. Today, a local legend about Skipton Castle includes a lurid account of how William then seized the lady of the lordship and forced her to marry him at sword point. This is a fantasy. The lady of Skipton was none other than Alice de Rumilly, sister of Avice de Rumilly and sister-in-law to the second William de Courcy of Stogursey. She was, therefore, also related to her sister's brother-in-law, Jordan de Courcy – she was John de Courcy's aunt.

William fitz Duncan was no wild marauding Scot. Although his ancestors included Scottish kings he also counted Normans amongst them and had grown up in the court of King Henry of England. Significantly, King David, before he succeeded to the Scottish throne, also spent considerable time at King Henry's court as a young aristocrat where, with William fitz Duncan, he was trained in Norman government, fighting and outlook. Rather than the fictional dramatic scene in the chapel of Skipton Castle in 1138, William fitz Duncan's marriage to Alice de Rumilly took place some years before and had been arranged by that practised schemer King Henry of England. It was just one more example of Henry's many moves by which aristocrats from outlying and bordering territories were interlinked with the Norman aristocracy of England. William fitz Duncan was as Norman as the Lacy family he defeated.

The real cause of this curious campaign was that, in the chaos of the civil war, the Lacy family had tried to grab control of Alice de Rumilly's inheritance of the honours of Skipton and Copeland. These had been her share of the inheritance from her father and brother. The Lacy family wanted Skipton because it would give them control of the Aire Gap, the only significant west–east pass through the Pennines. The Lacys held many manors either side of the Pennines, in the honour of Clitheroe in the west and the honour of Pontefract in the east. The Aire Gap linked the two and, if the Lacys could control it, they would become powerful regional lords. When William fitz Duncan defeated the Lacys at Clitheroe it was because he was fighting to secure his wife's inheritance, and the fact that no other great lord in the region ever disputed his actions shows they agreed with his move.

It was only after her husband had thrown out the thieving Lacy family from Skipton that Alice de Rumilly took up residence there with him. There was no Hollywood-style dramatic forced marriage, but rather a lord and his lady reclaiming what was rightfully theirs. After William fitz Duncan's death a few years later, Alice de Rumilly married Alexander Fitzgerald and continued to reside at Skipton. By that time, Jordan de Courcy had moved his family northwards to administer the Yorkshire estates of his brother, the second William de Courcy of Stogursey. Jordan's sons, particularly John de Courcy, grew up just a short way from his aunt's wide-ranging honours of Skipton and Copeland. Not only did that mean he could range widely over the territory and meet family tenants whose sons would later settle in Ulster, but he also grew up in a heady atmosphere of family history linked to the kings of Scotland and England.

In about 1153 the second William de Courcy of Stogursey regained control of his Yorkshire estates and moved his younger brother, Jordan, and his family northwards to act as his steward and manager. King Stephen died in 1154 and by agreement he was succeeded by the oldest son of the Empress Matilda, who became King Henry II of England. Richard de Courcy had died in the previous year and his widow, Alice née Paynel, was swiftly married to Robert de Gant, a member of a prominent Lincolnshire aristocratic family loyal to the new King Henry II. Her lands finally left Courcy control.

William fitz Duncan died in about 1153. His widow and their children remained in possession of Skipton for many years, retaining some of the soldiers of Galloway who had formed part of William fitz Duncan's original force. These formed a significant part of the castle guard and acted as military instructors for the next generation of young aristocratic warriors. Skipton was at the top of the young John de Courcy's list of places to visit for extended periods and it was here that he not only received military training but also gained detailed knowledge of the political situation in north-west England, south-west Scotland, the Isle of Man and, of course, Ulster.

In addition to part of the eastern Pennines, the lordship of Skipton also controlled Copeland, that part of Cumbria which faces across the northern Irish Sea towards the glens of Antrim and County Down. John travelled throughout Cumbria, staying with tenants of the lordship of Skipton, making friends, visiting local monasteries and constantly gaining knowledge and experience. It can be no surprise that when he made himself lord of Ulster, many of his new tenants were drawn from this territory and he made grants and foundations on behalf of monasteries stretching from near Carlisle to as far south as Chester. They had been founded by the same families with which the marriage of John's uncle William of Stogursey had created links. Moreover, Skipton, Copeland and Chester were not the only lordships in the region in which John was welcomed as a relation. Another of his cousins was Cecily, the daughter of William fitz Duncan, who married William the Fat, lord of Holderness and earl of York. When John de Courcy installed tenants in newly-conquered Ulster, they were drawn from these same areas. John's lordship of Ulster was a family business.

Ireland

John first visited Dublin in 1171. He was only a minor knight within the massive royal army with which King Henry overawed the Irish princes and brought Strongbow and the other Anglo-Norman adventurers in Ireland into line. John travelled with Robert Puher, one of the family that was now administering the lordship of Stogursey on the king's behalf, and they were almost certainly accompanied by John's brother, Jordan. Robert Puher is recorded as shipping cavalry equipment and other supplies for the king. While Henry was staying at Dublin in the special camp built just outside the city for the king and his army, John approached him and raised the subject of Ulster, far to the north and untouched by Norman incursions. As in the case of Philip de Braose, who received a royal grant for Limerick, King Henry laughingly granted Ulster to John "provided he could conquer it by force".

John cut an unlikely figure at the time; still somewhat inexperienced and with little personal following, but fired up with the idea of conquering the territory he had heard so much about as he had grown up in northern England. Henry could not have regarded John's request with much seriousness and the whole story might be just that, a story subsequently invented to justify the invasion. In later years it was certainly in Henry's interest to say that he had made the grant as, when John had indeed conquered Ulster, the king could then claim his own over-lordship and that John's status was simply that of his tenant in the north-east of Ireland. Whatever the truth of the story may be, John had the king's consent and now only needed the opportunity to have a go at turning it into reality. Eventually, his patience was rewarded.

He returned to Dublin in 1176 as part of the royal garrison under the command of King Henry II's newly-appointed administrator William fitz Aldelin. As a landless aristocratic warrior, John was following the career of a paid knight in the king's service, but loyalty to his lord went far beyond the latter's ability to pay. Gerald of Wales mentioned that John arrived in Dublin with two other captains who each commanded a force of about ten knights. John also commanded such a group, having gained his experience and acceptance as a leader of fighting men in the years since his father's death.

John had resorted to selling his sword wherever he could because what little prospects he might have had from his father had evaporated at just the moment he was entering adulthood. In 1171, the third William de Courcy, the lord of Stogursey and owner of the Yorkshire lands which John's father, Jordan, managed as his steward, died leaving only an infant son – also called William – as his heir. The infant William was John's nephew. As a result of the death of the third William de Courcy and because the Courcy family was a tenant-in-chief of the king, the royal government took over the running of the Stogursey lordship on behalf of the very young fourth William de Courcy. William le Puher and Hugh Pincerna, two important tenants of the Courcys in Somerset, were appointed by King Henry II's administration to manage the estates. If John's father, Jordan, was still alive at that time, he was relieved of his stewardship of the Courcy's northern estates and moved back to Middleton Cheney, although it is more likely that he also died at about this time. This left John de Courcy with a dilemma. He had inherited his father's modest manor but not the lucrative administration of the Courcys' northern estates.

These were poor prospects indeed for the young John and it is no wonder that he spent the next few years making his way as a penniless fighter, hiring himself out to whoever might need a knight's murderous abilities. The best employer was, of course, the king, as he always needed armed men to police his far-flung territories and to fight in his regular summer campaigns. Catching the king's eye was not easy, however, and John first had to build up that personal experience and expertise in warfare for which he was subsequently praised by contemporaries. John, together with his younger brother Jordan, naturally turned to the Courcy family for their initial employment. Clearly the lordship of Stogursey had no need for them, or at least was under the control of individuals whose only interest was in farming the estates on behalf of the king and, no doubt, for themselves, so they had to look elsewhere.

John turned to his cousins in Normandy. There, the senior branch of the family was headed by another William de Courcy but, unlike his namesakes in England, he held a post of considerable importance in the royal government of the duchy. William de Courcy of Courcy-sur-Dives was King Henry II's seneschal or steward of Normandy, responsible for the routine administration of the duchy, particularly the enforcement of royal rights and taxes, for which he accounted at the ducal Exchequer in Caen. His responsibility extended throughout Normandy and he needed a group of warriors ready to enforce the decisions of the courts and collect payment of all that was owed to the king. Here was an ideal environment for John and Jordan to gain employment and experience, and they were to spend the next five years in Normandy in the service of their cousin. Moreover, being in the household of the king's steward gave John opportunities to be noticed by the king's counsellors and perhaps by Henry II himself.

William de Courcy of Normandy died in 1176 and his job of ducal steward went to another family. His death closed off another avenue for John and yet again he was cast adrift. By this time, however, he had made a sufficiently favourable impression on the king or his counsellors to be appointed as part of the new royal garrison of Dublin. Being chosen to go to Ireland was no accident; John undoubtedly put himself forward for the post. He had had his sights set westwards from his teenage years when he first learned from his contacts in northern England and Galloway about the fragile political situation in Ulster and the tremendous potential that it offered to a determined and risk-taking adventurer such as himself. After all, he had very little to lose and all to gain by chancing his luck in Ireland.

Now, with plenty of fighting and organising experience behind him, John returned to Dublin as one of several captains subordinate to William fitz Aldelin. This, however, was only a stepping stone towards his ultimate objective. John was back in Ireland at the head of a force of men and with the leadership skills, personal charisma and authority to make good King Henry's jesting permission. For John, there was no time limit to the royal consent he had received in 1171 and now, at last, he had scraped together the resources to chance his luck. He was ready to gamble that Fortune's wheel would turn in his favour.

Gerald of Wales commented that the knights forming the Dublin garrison were dissatisfied with William fitz Aldelin's leadership. They expected him to raid the Irish kingdoms surrounding the Norman-controlled territory, even during winter. Instead, Gerald depicted their commander as acting deviously and seeking to buy off Irish opposition rather than confront it. Chafing at this relative inactivity, some of the knights were easily persuaded by John that there was honour and glory – and land – to be won away to the north of Norman Dublin. Thus it was that John was able to lead 22 knights northwards from the garrison. No Norman knight travelled alone. Each was accompanied by at least his squire and a groom to tend to his several horses. Moreover, John would have ensured that he included Norman infantry and archers in the force. In effect it was a small army in which all the necessary types of fighting troops needed to ensure mutual support in any battle were present. When John faced Dunlevy's attack at Downpatrick he commanded a small but proficient and powerful fighting force.

Downpatrick – the target

John de Courcy chose to attack in February 1177. Such a winter campaign was very unusual for the time. Normally armies would keep to their winter quarters with only small-scale foraging raids to relieve the tedium. John's objective was the native Irish hill fort of Down, modern-day Downpatrick's Hill of Down. This was the centre of the small Irish sub-kingdom of Dál Fiatach and of the over-kingdom of Ulaid, approximately those parts of Counties Antrim and Down east of the upper and lower river Bann and Lough Neagh. The Hill of Down was a typical hill-fort site. The cathedral now occupies the top of a rounded hill which is all but isolated from the surrounding high ground by areas which, until modern drainage schemes were built from the eighteenth century onwards, were frequently under water and were always marshy. Even today, the land either side of the river Quoile is liable to flooding. The land is low-lying on all but the eastern side, where an easily-defended narrow tongue of higher ground linked the hill fort with the rest of King Rory Mac Dunlevy's territory. It also controlled the river Quoile, which in this period was an important route way to much of eastern Down via Strangford Lough and, through the narrows, to the Irish Sea and beyond.

Downpatrick formed a secular settlement containing the ruling lord's house and household linked to a religious enclosure. Ecclesiastical activity on the site dates back to the fifth century, for the eighth-century monastery replaced an earlier Celtic Christian centre. Additionally, the local king had his administrative centre there, combining secular and religious activities in a characteristically Irish manner. By the early eleventh century the settlement had grown down the gently sloping eastward flank of the hill where the cathedral now stands. A medieval road heading north-east left Downpatrick from this point and met the river at what is now Quoile bridge. This was the site of a ferry which John de Courcy subsequently seized and granted to the monks of Downpatrick Cathedral. From the other side of the river bank the road then ran northwards towards Killyleagh. A number of ferries crossed both the river Quoile and Strangford Lough throughout this period and were a valuable source of income and control for whoever owned them. After his victory, John made good use of these ferries as valuable gifts to the monasteries he established, but kept the important and remunerative link between Strangford and Portaferry for himself. He granted the remainder to Downpatrick Abbey in 1180.

The name 'Quoile' comes from the Irish for narrow, cael, and refers to the navigable tidal channel where it joins Strangford Lough. Upstream, the river originally opened out and flooded much of the land either side at each high tide. Barriers built in the last 200 years have altered the lay of the land so that today's landscape is quite different. The barriers encouraged mud to build up on the landward side and, by reducing the river's width, speeded up its rate of flow which, in turn, deepened the channel. When John arrived in 1177, however, the area inland of the Quoile's narrow entry into Strangford was a substantial flooded area known as Lough Down, particularly noted for its salmon fishery. After his conquest, John granted all fishing rights along the narrow stretch of the river to Inch Abbey but gave the more substantial rights covering all of Lough Down to his new abbey dedicated to Saint Patrick built on the site of the Irish fort. It was John de Courcy who gave Downpatrick its name and began its long association with Ireland's patron saint.

John also began to build a motte-and-bailey castle at Downpatrick. This, now known as the Mound of Down, stands a short distance to the north of the cathedral. It is a natural outcrop adapted into a native Irish structure, perhaps as a secure site for King Dunlevy's most valuable cattle and his horses. After John's victory he began rebuilding the Mound as a castle so as to separate its secular administrative function from the religious centre which now occupied the whole of the Hill of Down. However, before it was completed, the need for a military and administrative post at Downpatrick receded and, instead, John developed his defences further afield with new castles, such as Dromore, while the centre of his new lordship became his magnificent stone keep at Carrickfergus.

John established his control of eastern County Down relatively quickly because he knew that in the past Downpatrick had needed its defences. It had been raided by Vikings in AD 942; the river Quoile gave these expert seamen an easy route to the settlement. Forty-seven years later, in AD 989, the Vikings returned, sacked the settlement at Downpatrick again and burned it to the ground. The wooden buildings were burnt yet again in the year 1111 when they were struck by lightning.

The nearby monastery of Inis Cumhscraigh completes the picture of Downpatrick at the time of John's victory. Like the Celtic Christian community long established on the Hill of Down, the monastery of Inis Cumhscraigh was founded in the eighth century and dedicated to the local Saint Mo Bíu of Inis Cúscraid. The Vikings raided the monastery in 1001 and took many prisoners. It was evidently prospering at that stage, but by 1177 it was all but abandoned. John subsequently revitalised the site, inviting Cistercian monks to his new foundation of Inch Abbey, the remains of which are still standing.

Overall, the area which King Dunlevy of Downpatrick controlled – the kingdom of Dál Fiatach – comprised a small but comparatively well-organised maritime territory with considerable resources, but bedevilled by factional divisions and dynastic rivalries within the ruling family. Its rich farmlands were productive, Lecale being noted for its grain production. John knew that it was not just a prize worth winning, it was also ripe for conquest. His plans were well researched and well organised. He did not just head north from the Dublin garrison on some vague whim, he knew exactly where he was going and the situation he would find there, for he had spent his teenage years in northern England amongst those who were knowledgeable about the lands across the Irish Sea.

The invasion of Ulster

In early February 1177, John's small army marched northwards for three days, passing through Meath. He arrived at Downpatrick just as dawn was breaking on the fourth morning. The Irish king, Dunlevy, was taken completely by surprise. He had not rallied his forces and so immediately fled with the few troops he had with him. He had not been warned by any of the Irish kings who had allowed John to pass through their territory.

They were evidently either bought off by John, promised some future reward or were pleased to see Dunlevy attacked. After all, if John failed, the warfare would weaken Dunlevy and make him an easy target for others. If John succeeded he might not be strong enough to hold all of Dunlevy's territory and, again, others could grab some of the land. Furthermore, John gained some Irish soldiers en route to add to his army. These were either provided by the Irish kings holding territory on his march from Dublin to Downpatrick or were recruited as mercenaries. In either case the Irish kings were keen for John and his men to pass quickly through their territory, they had no wish to confront a Norman army, no matter how modest its size.

John's decision to campaign in the middle of winter was extremely unusual for the time. Food stocks were getting low, the weather was bad and the days still short. The Dublin garrison was discontented, although this is hardly a rare situation amongst soldiers, but John's timing wasn't just dependent on his fellow knights' grumbling over their inactivity. Instead, he specifically chose this time because winter campaigns were so rare and unexpected and, just as he hoped, he was able to surprise his enemy at the very time when they least expected an attack. It was typical of John's leadership. He utilised every possible advantage to its greatest extent.

Having captured Downpatrick without a fight, John's small invading foreign army seized booty and supplies and dug themselves in, knowing that their easy victory would soon be hotly contested by the Irish keen to defend their land. Amongst the plunder, John captured the visiting papal legate, Vivian, who now attempted to negotiate a settlement. In accordance with Irish custom, Dunlevy offered John an annual tribute if he would leave but this didn't suit the Normans at all. Firstly, it's very unlikely that they would have been able to collect on the promise once they left and, secondly and more importantly, they wanted land, not cash. The principal aim of John's elite aristocratic knights was to seize foreign territory, settle on it themselves, create estates, install tenants, marry the sisters and daughters of other invading Normans and establish their own dynasty. They were land-hungry. They wanted medieval society's primary resource on which to create lordships and establish their status amongst their fellow aristocrats. Dunlevy's aim was to recapture the land from which he had been driven. Their aims were irreconcilable. A battle was inevitable.

The opposing armies

Dunlevy rallied his forces and attacked. A Norman monk, Gerald of Wales, writing a few years later, claimed that the Irish fought naked and unarmed, believing it a sign of bravery. This is untrue, of course, but it does demonstrate their great valour. Gerald probably meant that they fought without the chain mail armour worn by the Normans. He described the weapons which the Irish used. These were darts, short spears and axes. Significantly, he did not list archers, which seems strange as the technology was far from new. Instead, the Irish used their darts and short spears as missiles and in mêlées. Their use of axes was relatively new in the twelfth century, having been learnt from Viking raiders and settlers. Gerald stressed the Irish fighters' speed and ability to use anything, even stones, as missiles against their enemies. They did not have cavalry as a fighting unit although some might have travelled to battle on horseback.

By contrast, the surviving sources, primarily the account of the extremely partisan Gerald of Wales, depict the Normans as "naturally" superior, "better fighters" and "more civilised" than the Irish. It's not surprising that this Norman monk should present such a biased view in favour of his fellow countrymen. Gerald was a member of the extended Fitzgerald family which played a major role in King Henry II's invasion of Ireland in the twelfth century and its subsequent rule by the Anglo-Normans of England. John's army, "although small in numbers, was of excellent calibre", and equipped and trained for a very different type of warfare to the shout-and-charge technique of the Irish. As with all armies, both the Irish and the Normans relied on personal valour, esprit-de-corps and individual élan, but the core of John's army comprised men-at-arms led by his handful of dismounted knights. These well-armoured and armed heavy infantry formed the centre of his position and John's intention was that they would receive the force of the initial Irish attack and stand firm without being overwhelmed or flinching back.

John's heavy infantry were supported by lightly-armed Irish mercenaries or allies which he had recruited on his northwards march. They were used as a protective screen in front of the Norman infantry to help disrupt the Irish attack and then fall back to stand alongside the core of John's force and protect their flanks. In addition, the Normans had archers. Initially, these were deployed in advance of the infantry so as to get the maximum range in firing on the advancing Irish. As soon as the attackers came close, however, the archers withdrew behind the infantry and continued to fire over their heads until the front ranks crashed together. The Norman archers were a valuable part of John's forces and he paid careful attention to their deployment. His force was drawn up on the north-west facing side of the Hill of Down, just below the site of the cathedral, forcing the Irish to attack uphill and also allowing him to send his archers further up the rise behind his front line after the Irish came close. In this position, John's archers were able to use their added height to achieve greater range and rain arrows down on the unengaged Irish fighters towards the rear of the attacking force, further encouraging disorganisation and panic.

The most important element of John's army were the young aristocratic knights who, like him, were seeking to conquer permanent lordships within Ulster. They formed an elite unit of characteristic Norman heavy cavalry clad in chain mail and carrying one or more spears for throwing or charging, and a long battle sword for close combat. They were shock troops combining speed, greater height compared to a foot soldier, and the psychological advantage of a charging cavalry force. Once stopped, however, they became vulnerable to attack by soldiers on foot. John personally led his small group of cavalrymen. They were each well-mounted on their best battle horses and had the support of several of their own squires and grooms, who stood ready with fresh horses to replace killed, injured or winded chargers. Initially, John kept the horses well to the rear in the battle's early stages, up slope and protected, while he and his fellow aristocrats first fought dismounted alongside his men-at-arms.

Gerald of Wales described the Irish army as numbering ten thousand but it would be more accurate to think of Dunlevy's forces as being 'a lot', certainly many more than John could muster to defend his position. Undoubtedly, the Irish outnumbered John's army but the principal aim of Gerald's exaggeration was to depict his fellow Normans as heroic and steadfast against overwhelming odds and also to depict John and his men in a David-and-Goliath struggle. Consequently, the great bravery of the Irish soldiers in crossing over a river and marshes and then attacking uphill while under attack from archers and spear-throwers is barely mentioned in this partisan account.

John had not been idle since seizing Downpatrick. He had ordered his men to build a temporary fort within the wide-ranging ramparts at the top of the hill, where John founded the cathedral. His fort was planned to prevent surreptitious incursions and thefts as well as to provide security for John's foreign invading force in the midst of Irish territory. Rapidly-built, it was designed for routine defence, but not to forestall an army. It could not withstand a siege. John had not had much of a chance to amass a stockpile of food and his enclosure did not contain a source of fresh water. He was isolated in a foreign country controlled by the hostile Irish keen to defend their own land. Lastly, but most importantly, the circuit around the top of the Hill of Down – Cathedral Hill – was far too long for John to defend, as it would require him to spread his forces very thinly.

The hill fort did not suit the Anglo-Normans' method of waging war nor was it a position that could be adequately defended. To be victorious, John needed to fight the Irish on land of his choosing and on his terms. The Anglo-Norman army required room to fight. Its cavalry could only be effective on firm ground and with a sufficient distance to build up to a gallop for a crushing shock assault, if required. Similarly, the armoured men-at-arms and lighter infantry needed to deploy on good ground. Ideally, this would have a slight downward slope towards the enemy, so as to give each man sufficient space in which to fight and to raise them higher than the attackers. The Normans did not use the compact shield wall of tightly-packed heavy infantry characteristic of the Saxons defeated at Hastings a century earlier. They needed room to swing their swords. Such an open formation, in which each relied on his compatriots on either side, could only be achieved through discipline, experience and trust, and this the Normans at Downpatrick had in abundance. Whether it was justified or not, it was the cornerstone of their own sense of superiority.

In addition, the Anglo-Norman archers also needed space to fight. They would be much less effective tightly packed into a confined fort. Their strength lay in their ability to produce rapid missile fire with arrows landing on the enemy, in flight, and about to be fired. In addition, they could move to new positions as quickly as a running man. A competent commander could use this flexibility to bring their firepower down on the enemy wherever it was needed. Moreover, apart from such responsiveness, archers could keep a retreating enemy in range by following up as they fell back or ran away. John used his archers very efficiently at Downpatrick.

The Battle of Downpatrick

Eight days after fleeing from Downpatrick, King Rory Mac Dunlevy returned with his army ready for battle. His aim was to destroy John and his army. It would achieve nothing if all he succeeded in doing was to force them away in good order because the Normans would remain together as a threatening fighting force. Consequently, Dunlevy wanted to engage them in combat; he wanted the battle and was prepared to attack them in their prepared position so as to destroy them. Moreover, his Irish soldiers were keen to drive these land-grabbing foreigners from their territory.

John led his forces out of their small enclosure on the flatter ground at the top of the Hill of Down onto the sloping side. This placed the Normans well above the soft marshland which spread out on either side of the river Quoile. John positioned his men on the north-west flank of the hill, facing out towards Dunlevy's forces as they approached. The Irish had to ford the river, cross the marshy area on its edge and only then begin their attack uphill. John hoped the boggy ground around the hill would help protect his army's flanks and limit the chances of it being surrounded by the much larger Irish army. He also expected it to slow down and disorganise the Irish troops. He placed his most powerful troops in the centre of his defensive line. These comprised his knights fighting on foot at this stage of the battle and his men-at-arms. He positioned himself right in the centre – John always chose the most prominent place for himself in any battle, and it was usually the most dangerous. On either flank he deployed his lighter troops, including those from his Irish allies. No doubt each flank curved slightly round and up the hill so as to limit the possibility of being outflanked. John read the terrain well, using his long experience as a soldier, and utilised the best position for his troops.

This position also restricted the frontage against which the Irish could attack and thereby reduced the importance of their numerical advantage. Their objective was to get into hand-to-hand fighting with the Normans and destroy them. Dunlevy could not allow any part of John's forces to survive as they would withdraw, regroup and could attack again another day. Several factors encouraged Dunlevy to make a frontal assault up the hill. First and foremost he wished to engage and defeat John, not chase him away. Secondly, honour and glory was won by attacking an enemy face-to-face and defeating him; and finally this form of direct attack was that most commonly used by Irish armies. It demonstrated the bravery of the Irish soldiers. Dunlevy's army was comprised of separate elements each commanded by their own local lord and they competed for the honour of confronting the enemy's leadership. Thus, once Dunlevy had unleashed the characteristic Irish battle charge he would have no control of his forces and certainly could not have diverted any section into a flanking attack. He would know that every one of his supporters would be aiming to kill John de Courcy and the other invaders.

Gerald's description of the battle was written some years after the event and when he had spent some time as a guest of John de Courcy. It was designed to show the valour of the Normans and their skill at winning the victory. An important aspect of the account was the way in which he presented the Irish as well-armed, brave and in much greater numbers than his heroes. By presenting the attackers in this way, Gerald's aim was to add lustre to his compatriots' success, even if his description of events owed more to his imagination and the oft-repeated stories of those who fought and won on the day. For example, Gerald said that both sides used similar weapons. This is an unlikely claim, especially as he had described the quite different Irish weapons earlier in his book. Also although he recounted that both sides met in hand-to-hand combat he reserved all of his praise for the Normans and ignored the courage of the Irish.

As Dunlevy's forces approached the Hill of Down and crossed the marshy meadows either side of the Quoile river, John de Courcy's archers began firing at them, inflicting death and injury even at some distance. This angered Dunlevy's men, as it would any attacking force, as they were suffering injuries and casualties without being able to attack the enemy. As a result they bravely sought to speed up their attack so as to get close to the Normans. To do so they would have to make an heroic charge up what is even today quite a steep slope. Their battle charge would force the Norman archers to stop firing and run back behind John's battle line for protection.

The Irish battle charge made a fearsome sight rushing up the hill towards the small Anglo-Norman army. Although to John and his men it may have looked disorganised, in fact the Irish soldiers could use this tactic with deadly effect. They fought alongside men they had known all their lives and were led by their traditional tribal leaders. They recognised each other and, although divided into separate units according to the territory from which they came, each of those apparently disorganised forces were self-supporting and could react flexibly to any battle situation. They were a formidable force. John's men needed all their courage to stand and face the attack for, unlike a battle fought on level ground, the Normans could see the entire strength of the attacking army spread out before them. It must have been a chilling sight.

Nevertheless, even at this stage of the battle the psychological advantage wasn't all in favour of the Irish. In addition to the Norman archers' constant firing, as the Irish got within range, John's foot soldiers let fly with spears and other missiles to further blunt the attack. Those foot soldiers included some Irish light infantry which John had recruited either near Dublin or en route to Downpatrick and, although lightly armed and unlikely to hold their ground against Dunlevy's battle charge, they had long experience at fighting other Irish war bands and best knew how to make the most of their spears.

The attacking Irish would have felt very exposed crossing the marshy water meadows up towards the Hill of Down. The waterlogged ground slowed down their progress and, as Gerald commented, the Normans' archery had a devastating impact. It was a grim advance across bad ground with compatriots repeatedly struck down and left for dead. Furthermore, as they reached firmer footing at the base of the hill they then faced ground that rose comparatively steeply to the more level terrain at the summit. Dunlevy's only hope was to rally his men as they neared the Normans and encourage them to launch a powerful assault. With a mighty shout his Irish warriors thrust forward to crash onto the line of knights and men-at-arms which formed the core and centre of John de Courcy's small army. It was a brave action. Dunlevy's aim was to break the enemy's organisation with this single crashing attack and, against Irish armies, it usually worked and delivered the knockout blow. This time, however, the Irish faced a different sort of army and, most important of all, John de Courcy was in its front rank.

John's tactic was simple. Recognising that the strength of an Irish army lay in the impact of this first attack, he organised his forces so they would be as well placed as possible to receive the blow and stand firm. The physical and psychological impact of that blow was what made Irish armies successful in battle against each other. For John, therefore, the strength of his army lay in its ability to hold their ground, keep its position and maintain its organisation and discipline against that shock. At all costs he sought to avoid his fighting line of heavy infantry from disintegrating into disorganised hand-to-hand fighting, which the Irish troops behind the front line could then move into and deploy their numerical strength. The crisis point came right at the beginning of the battle as Dunlevy's fiercely charging Irish soldiers crashed into the Normans' line. Would it hold? The whole battle, the whole future of these men, of John de Courcy and of their conquest of Ulster, hung in the balance.

The Normans fought fiercely without flinching or breaking ranks. They withstood the fearless Irish attack, brought it to a juddering stop and, as the brutal close fighting continued, their experience, mutual co-operation and protective chain mail tunics began to give them the upper hand. They kept together and aided each other rather than letting the engagement become chaotic. Gerald, of course, only recounts the heroism of the Normans and ignores that of the Irish. When he said that "there were many who behaved bravely in this battle" he was only referring to the invading Normans. One of these was Roger Poher, a young man from the Somerset family who were tenants of the Courcys of Stogursey. He was "a youth as yet unbearded, fair-haired, handsome and tall", and he particularly distinguished himself in the combat. Roger not only fought for his life and those of his compatriots, he was also fighting for Irish land, for the chance to carve out an estate so that he could become a powerful tenant of a mighty lord. His example was repeated along the ranks of the Normans who fought that day at Downpatrick to conquer Ulster for this new foreign elite.

After some minutes of fierce fighting it became clear that John and his men had successfully halted the fearsome Irish attack. The Normans had succeeded in stopping the terrifying assault. Those Irish further back who were not yet fighting John's men pressed forward so as to get in close to their enemy. They wanted to move up so as to show their valour in the battle and also to escape the continuing attack of the Norman archers who were firing over the heads of their own men and into the attacking mass charging up from lower down the hill. However, brave as it was, the Irish attack had stalled and bloody butchery was taking place, as the more powerfully-armed Normans took every opportunity to slice down Dunlevy's men.

At this stage, only a few minutes into the actual fighting, the Irish position had already become dangerous. Stopped at the front, beaten by the Norman knights and men-at-arms, pressed from the rear by those trying to get up and away from the archers' arrows, the whole force began to degenerate into confusion. Gerald stresses that after the initial Irish battle charge had faltered and begun to fall back, each man looked to his own and his friends survival. Dunlevy's army comprised men from the different kin groups within his kingdom and, as their king's leadership began to be seen as unsuccessful, these groups looked to their own.

The attack had ground to a halt and failed. Now the Irish were to pay for their inability to break the Normans' line. They quickly realised they were in a dangerous position and their morale began to plummet. By contrast, that of the Normans rose rapidly. They had stopped the massive Irish attack in its tracks, they stood firm on their chosen ground and the enemy was beginning to falter. The Irish at the front were beginning to break off the fight and fall back down the slope, adding to the chaos caused by those further back still pressing forward. As soon as they broke from the Normans, John's archers had them in their sights once more, while his lighter troops could again use spears and other missiles to add to the slaughter.

John was in a good position to assess the situation. His army's small frontage meant that he could easily see what was going on in the battle and he could assess the remaining strength of the knights and other soldiers who were fighting alongside him. Looking down the slope of the hill and seeing the Irish falling back he immediately recognised that his opportunity for a complete victory had arrived and he responded in a characteristically Norman way. Leaving the armoured men-at-arms to slowly move forward when ready, he called his small band of knights together and instructed the squires to bring forward their war horses. Quickly, his group of elite aristocratic Norman cavalrymen formed up, re-equipped with fresh armaments where necessary and, at John's command and with a blood-curdling yell, charged down the slope at the backs of the retreating Irish. It was the terrifying coup-de-grace for Dunlevy's men.

Glancing over their shoulders, the Irish saw heavily-armoured Norman cavalrymen charging towards them as they retreated down the hill and into the boggy meadows. The sight caused panic amongst the Irish soldiers. The psychological impact was tremendous for, although John and his men numbered only a couple of dozen, their charge was completely unexpected and they were the last thing the withdrawing Irishmen wished to turn and face. No doubt there were more than enough Irish soldiers to stop and destroy these few cavalrymen but they had lost the organisation and, more importantly, the morale to rally, turn and stand their ground to defeat them. Within a few moments the massive Irish army had charged, been stopped and forced to retreat. Then, like avenging demons, the Normans had unleashed their terrifying heavy cavalry against them – a type of fighting force which they had never faced before.

Now the battle turned into slaughter. The first of the retreating Irish were caught in the soft ground of the Quoile's floodplain. This slowed their flight and added to the confusion. John reined in his cavalry before they got into the bog – he had prepared for the battle and knew the ground well. John had used the shock effect of the Norman cavalry brilliantly. It was a tactical masterpiece. Trained from youth, his fellow knights controlled their equally well-trained horses with precision. The Norman archers moved forward, protected by John's foot soldiers, and continued to rain down death on the Irish. As Dunlevy's army quickly collapsed into a disorganised mass, John's foot soldiers moved closer to complete their destruction and, in particular, John's Irish allies seized this opportunity to destroy and loot. It was a frightful sight.

Even writing years later Gerald of Wales vividly conjures up the scene, saying that a "great number of the enemy were killed along the sea shore where they had taken refuge"; the sea shore being the banks of the tidal Quoile. Gerald then quotes Saint Columbkille's prophecy that the slaughter "would be so great that their enemies would wade up to their knees in their blood" and continues "the weight of their bodies caused men to sink deep into [the soft ground], and the blood pouring from their wounds remained on the surface of the slippery ground and easily came up to the knees and legs of their pursuers".

The battle was over. Dunlevy was defeated and humiliated. He had lost his kingdom to this upstart Norman. Battles didn't last long in the twelfth century and this one was particularly quick. In February in County Down sunrise is at about 8.00 am. If Dunlevy moved to attack shortly after the mists had risen then the probable time for the fighting is about mid-morning. The battle didn't last long so John's forces had most of the short winter's day to chase the defeated Irish. He rallied his men an hour or two before dusk, which was at about 5.00 pm, and they withdrew back into their temporary fort to tend their wounds, bury their dead and, most of all, celebrate their victory. The Normans remained watchful, however, as they knew that Dunlevy would make more attempts against them. Nevertheless, it took the Irish king several months to rally sufficient men and attempt to win back his kingdom. On 24 July he returned to Downpatrick with what Gerald claims to have been an even bigger army but was once again defeated. In fact, John was not just victorious for a second time, he was by this stage becoming undisputed master of all of Ulster east of the river Bann, north and south of Lough Neagh, and, like any successful war leader, he attracted men and allies to his side. Success led to more success and by the end of the year he was the unchallenged Prince of Ulster.

Lord of Ulster

We know what John de Courcy looked like because he was described by Gerald of Wales, a churchman who stayed with the lord of Ulster sometime in the 1180s. Gerald mentions that John had his own historians who would record his exploits more fully, but unfortunately those other accounts have not survived. Nevertheless, Gerald's description is vivid and lets us picture what the new Prince of Ulster was like. John was tall and fair-haired, and had bony and sinewy limbs. He had great bodily strength, a very strong physique and an extraordinarily bold temperament. He was courageous from his youth and a skilful warrior. As an aristocrat he was, of course, quite literally born to be a fighter and a proficient soldier. He was always at the centre of the fighting, even to the extent of rushing into the fray when he should hold back and direct operations. Perhaps his one flaw was his willingness to put himself into dangerous situations. Gerald criticised this, saying that he abandoned a leader's self control and, in a headstrong manner, made for the heart of the action. He was valorous and impetuous, brave and fiercesome. Over the years, John got into several close scrapes when campaigning outside his lordship because he was always at the sharpest point of conflict and committed himself to battle without hesitation. Gerald describes him at the Battle of Downpatrick wielding his sword with deadly accuracy, lopping off the heads, arms and hands of his adversaries. To his fellow Normans and the native Irish within his lordship he was a charismatic leader and a much-feared warrior.

John was also a good propagandist. He made sure that Gerald of Wales' book, *The Conquest of Ireland*, included Saint Columbkille's prophecy of the bloody scene on the shores of the river Quoile. Gerald's account includes the saint's prediction that a poor and needy man, a fugitive from other lands, would arrive at Down with a small force, take possession of the place and disdain the authority of any superior lord. If Gerald's account of the prophecy is accurate then it was tailor-made for John, especially as his actions in the Dublin garrison laid him open to all sorts of charges of disloyalty and disobedience to the king of England. He was certainly poor and needy, having no significant land of his own, and he never regarded himself as under the authority of another if he could possibly avoid it.

John also drew Gerald's attention to the prophecy of Silvester of Celidon. In that, again according to Gerald, John matched the saint's vision that a man, mounted on a white horse and with eagle emblems on his shield, would capture Ulaid. Gerald stressed John's fair hair, "tending in fact towards white", identifying it with Silvester's prediction of a white knight. Also, luckily for John, he 'chanced' to be riding a white horse at Downpatrick – or at least that is the way he remembered it. To complete the accuracy of the saintly prediction, John's shield carried the Courcy family crest of three eagles, rampant. John may have gathered these prophecies himself in preparation for Gerald's visit and drew them to the writer's attention. John was no fool and knew the power of such visions.

Initially, Downpatrick was established as John's capital. He granted all of the former king's fort on the Hill of Down to the Church and dedicated the site to Saint Patrick. John initially transferred his own secular authority to his partially-built motte-and-bailey fortress nearby, overlooking the site of his greatest victory, but he built his most important castle at Carrickfergus. This became the centre of his lordship, his caput. The changes at Downpatrick removed the hill from secular authority and presented any Irish lord with the problem of placating the Church if he sought to defeat John and re-establish it as a king's settlement. The grant was a substantial act of patronage and won John the support of local churchmen. In particular, it united the Church's regional interests with those of John himself and established a mutually-beneficial relationship with Bishop Malachy III of Down.

Subsequently, the remains of Saint Patrick, Saint Brigid and Saint Columbkille were miraculously discovered in what was then described as the city of

Downpatrick. In 1186, John arranged for the remains to be reverently moved to the cathedral site where they would be tended by the Benedictine monks established there by John's patronage. The ceremony of translation was conducted under the auspices of the papal legate Cardinal Vivian and included important secular lords, with John de Courcy being the most prominent. As a result, Downpatrick Cathedral became the destination for pilgrimages, especially to visit the final resting place of Saint Patrick. The saint's immense popularity and association with Ireland owes much to John's promotion through patronage and publication.

John was especially generous to the Church. He revived the Celtic monastery of Inis Cumhscraigh on the north bank of the Quoile by granting its site, land and possessions to the Cistercians for the establishment of Inch Abbey. All grants to the Church would have been made as acts of pious penitence, but that which established Inch Abbey was especially important to John. The new abbey looked out across the Quoile to the site of John's victory in which so many men on both sides were killed. It was established partly to atone for the killings which the Normans had committed. In this action, John demonstrated that he was copying William the Conqueror's establishment of Battle Abbey on the site of his victory over King Harold at Hastings, 111 years earlier. Moreover, penitence aside, its foundation and position would have clearly demonstrated to his contemporaries that John was comparing himself favourably to the Normans' greatest war leader. He felt he was as triumphant as the conqueror of England.

Once the battles were won, John set about turning military success into feudal settlement. He did not sweep the Irish from the land he had conquered. In fact, the situation was the reverse. John wished the indigenous Irish to remain and to continue to farm the land, for it would have had no value to the new lord of Ulster without people to work it. As in England after 1066, the native people remained once their previous rulers had been defeated and they were now ruled and were loyal to a new foreign elite. However, many aspects did change, particularly the reorganisation of the land into Norman-style feudal manors suitable for this new elite.

John's method of making a feudal settlement was the same as that used by William the Conqueror after he captured England a century before. John rewarded his knights and other followers who had been at the battle with large tracts of land. He also encouraged new settlers to come to him in Ireland from those lordships in England with which he was personally connected. This was how John built up his own lordship. He needed tenants to become lords of the new manors which he set about creating. These tenants became the backbone of his control of Ulster. They turned out as mounted knights when he went to war and brought with them their under-tenants as men-at-arms. John's tenants administered the localities, policed and protected the peasantry, administered justice, farmed the land and gave loyalty to their lord. With John, they set about building motte-and-bailey castles throughout eastern Ulster.

The castles, many of which can still be seen in Down and Antrim, were first built as simple wooden ringworks on top of earthen mounds. They were hardly cutting-edge military technology in twelfth-century England, but were well suited to this newly-conquered territory in Ireland and were an effective defence against any hostile Irish. Later, some were replaced with stone forts. Today, they are hard to miss. For example, Dromore, Donaghadee and Clough Castles are characteristically Norman motte-and-bailey types and even the remains of the motte at Dundonald show John's handiwork. Overall, John built or adapted about 75 castles and defended sites, and all but a handful are east of the Upper and Lower Bann, the core of John's lordship. Sorting out some sites is difficult, however, as some were originally Irish forts or later became so after Ulster was reconquered by the Irish centuries later. Much of Dundrum Castle, for example, was rebuilt by the MacGuinness family.

Understanding what John's castles represented is crucial to understanding his lordship. The defeated Saxons described William the Conqueror's castles in post-conquest England as a mesh of chain mail, controlling the country with an iron fist imposing draconian rule over a demoralised population. This is the view of the defeated. Such accounts were written by monks who were younger sons or brothers of the aristocratic Saxon lords defeated at Hastings. Castles were not islands of power surrounded by a sea of hostility and potential insurrection. Today, their structure and military purpose is obvious, but this neglects their other functions. Rather than following Hollywood's fantasies and comparing them with US cavalry forts set amongst native Americans, a more accurate parallel would be modern local government offices combined with a police station. They had a military purpose, of course, but their principal role was administration and justice.

In Ulster, John and his leading tenants built castles to administer the territory as well as defend it. The new lord of Ulster had no need to advertise his wealth and power; it was self-evident in his conquests. His castles' administrative role extended over the surrounding population, their military role was to defend local resources, including the native population, against attacks from beyond the lordship. They did not provide a safe bastion from which marauding Norman rulers rode out to terrorise the Irish tenants and labourers in the locality. Quite the reverse, they were designed to provide a base from which the Norman defenders of that territory could operate against neighbouring hostile Irish lords. John's castles protected his most vital asset after the land: the local Irish peasantry. Without their daily toil no crops were sown and harvested, no animals were husbanded, no smithies worked and no wealth was created, and what was true for John was also true for his tenants. Far from brooding menacingly over a local population crushed under its military superiority, the local castle was a source of reassurance, security, justice and active defence. It demonstrated what every peasant sought: a reliable lord who could defend his territory and his tenants from attack and offer laws and justice to make everyday life as safe and secure as possible.

Carrickfergus

John de Courcy's capital in Ulster was his magnificent castle at Carrickfergus. It was a statement of his power and wealth, announcing to the world that this region was ruled by a strong and forthright aristocratic warrior. John positioned his castle so that it could be seen from anywhere on Belfast Lough and the surrounding countryside. Nothing like it had existed in Ulster prior to John's conquest: Irish buildings were single-storey wooden and daub structures. Carrickfergus Castle proclaimed a new era: the era of the Prince of Ulster.

Unlike John's other castles, which were first built of wood on top of an earth mound surrounded by a lower raised platform and ditch, Carrickfergus Castle was built of stone from the start and on an outcrop of basalt rock.

It comprised the square central keep and inner curtain wall of the castle we see today, and was subsequently surrounded by later walls and a gateway. Its location gets its name from King Fergus, son of Eric of Armoy. In Irish, Carrickfergus is Carraig Fheargus, the Rock of Fergus. King Fergus went from Ireland to conquer land in Scotland sometime in the early sixth century. Apparently in the year 531 he fell ill and returned to east Antrim to get a cure from a holy well. Unfortunately, Fergus was never cured, instead his ship foundered on rocks and he was drowned, leaving his name to the spot where he met his end.

Fergus's holy well is located down on the lough shore at Carrickfergus, almost in the sea, and John de Courcy selected this site to build his new castle, directly on top of this supply of pure water. A good source of water was essential to any castle and the reliability of the holy well was a major factor in John's choice of location. Undoubtedly, the quality of the water was the reason why the well was venerated by the Irish. They believed it magical that a well of pure water could be at a place almost in the salty lough. The position of the castle offered John many strategic advantages but, ever with an eye on local legend and belief, by incorporating the holy well into his new castle he also exploited the prestige of a religiously significant site and demonstrated to everyone that he was a powerful enough person to control it. John wanted to use every possible advantage to impress his new Irish tenantry and peasants, and secure his rule over them after his initial conquest. Building his new castle directly over a venerated holy well was a brilliant propaganda move.

The new lord of Ulster began work on Carrickfergus Castle in 1178 as soon as he had secured most of County Down and southern County Antrim. The castle grew rapidly on its tough basalt base and eventually comprised a substantial square keep attached to a larger polygonal wall, all built of stone. Perched on top of the rocks, the view from the top of the keep is excellent. The flat waters of the lough mean ships can be seen while they are still miles away, whilst the surrounding countryside is laid out in a panorama. John's new castle at Carrickfergus was very obvious to anyone standing anywhere around Belfast Lough or travelling by boat.

The site projects out into the lough and provided a natural moat and strong defensive position. Ships could tie up next to the castle, but potential attackers from the sea would have faced a tough time scaling the curtain wall. John placed the original entrance to the castle in the eastern side of the wall. This reduced the chance of an attack from the northern landward side because it forced any enemies to make their way around the base of the wall to the eastern side, or attempt the very dangerous option of climbing over a defended wall. The rocky connection to the shore was the only significantly vulnerable part of the curtain wall, so John had a ditch dug into the hard basalt to complete the moat on all four sides, at least at high tide. Access was by a drawbridge permanently staffed by John's soldiers, which could be raised for greater protection.

The sea and navigable rivers were the motorways of the medieval world. The inhabitants of the British Isles were skilled sailors many centuries before the advent of the Vikings and their fast-moving boats. The sea was the quickest means of transport and linked up what appear to us to have been isolated coastal settlements. Normans such as John de Courcy proudly remembered their own distant Viking ancestry and readily appreciated the importance of shipping and the control of the sea.

Carrickfergus Castle dominated Belfast Lough, historically known as Carrick Lough. By controlling this virtual inland sea, largely protected from the worst of the weather, John dominated the whole region because the lough and the river Lagan provided a route reaching almost to the western border of his lordship. It was John's own mare nostrum, and Carrickfergus Castle was the key to that control. The high quality of the construction of the keep and surrounding curtain wall illustrates the castle's importance to John's hold over his lordship.

John based some of his ships at the mouth of the river Bann, north of Coleraine, and others at Carrickfergus. John used his ships to patrol the lough as well as for trading. He controlled those who entered and left his territory, and exacted tribute or a tithe of their goods. If you wanted to trade in any Norman lordship you had to make sure the lord got his share. From the upper floors of the castle John's men maintained a watch over Belfast Lough and signalled the launch of their lord's ships to intercept any unknown or unwanted intruder. Being situated at the water's edge did not isolate the castle. It protected ships loading saleable local produce such as skins, and unloading imported supplies, such as wine, and, as a result, a settlement quickly grew up inland of the castle. Moreover, as with Inch Abbey, John's positioning of Carrickfergus Castle on the lough shore suggests that to some extent he was again copying that greatest of Norman heroes, William the Conqueror.

After conquering England in 1066, William the Conqueror began the construction of the Tower of London. His castle, the White Tower, was a massive square keep clad in cream limestone from Caen in Normandy. This was polished to make it reflect the sunlight and must have been dazzling on a bright day. It was located at the eastern edge of the city of London, England's most important port, so all trading ships on the river Thames had to pass by. This allowed him to control the trade of his new capital and it was also an ever-present and very visible reminder to the Londoners of his rule over the kingdom. Not only was it a dramatically cream coloured fortress, it also towered over the surrounding buildings.

In a similar way, John's castle at Carrickfergus not only effectively controlled trade along the principal route into his new lordship, it also stood out as a demonstration and reminder to everyone travelling through the lough of his power and prestige. His massive square keep was a statement of his lordship over all the land that could be seen by anyone travelling by boat. It was the biggest building in Ulster and towered over the surrounding Irish houses which grew into the town of Carrickfergus. John was saying to everyone who saw his castle that he owned everything the eye could see and the centre was this powerful stone fortress. Even today it stands out on the shoreline. Carrickfergus Castle is another example of the astute and flamboyant way in which John presented himself and his rule to the indigenous population and everyone who entered his lordship.

The castle was also John's administrative centre and his main residence, as well as a statement of aristocratic prestige. The central square keep has massive dimensions. The walls are almost 4 metres thick and around 40 metres high. John divided the keep into four floors connected by a spiral staircase The entrance was a door in the first floor. The ground floor was used for storage and had no doors or windows to make it vulnerable to attack.

The first floor provided quarters for the garrison and a medieval toilet within the garderobe. When John built the keep's walls he included a small alcove within their thickness. The alcove formed part of an internal room in the castle and was partitioned off with wooden walls.

Inside this garderobe there was a stone seat with a hole cut; this went down vertically and outwards through the walls to the outside. It emptied into the sea, and was washed away with each high tide. The garderobe was a high-status fitting in a castle. Houses in the twelfth century did not include indoor plumbing. John was again demonstrating his aristocratic status by incorporating a garderobe in his castle. As it contained a privy it was also used to hang clothing, such as coats and cloaks. People of the time believed that the smell of ammonia from the toilet would protect the clothing from vermin, and drive out fleas.

Carrickfergus Castle fulfilled a variety of functions in addition to its military purpose. John built the second floor as a single large room which could be used for private meetings and discussions as well as more formal public events. The most important function of the room for his tenantry was as a court where John and his stewards could settle disputes and investigate criminal acts. There was no distinction between civil and criminal law in the twelfth century. As the new lord of Ulster, John applied Norman law for his new leading tenants and, again imitating William the Conqueror, traditional Irish Brehon law for his lesser tenants and peasants. In any dispute between the new settlers and the established Irish, however, John applied Norman law, as was the practice in England. The room was also where John's officials received payments of rent from his leading

Norman tenants: usually a proportion of the produce of the various manors which they had been granted.

The large and airy top floor room, the solar, was John's private quarters where he and Affreca lived and so was the most socially-important part of the castle. It contained all of the couple's best clothing, valuable jewellery and other high-status items such as plate and drinking vessels. It also acted as a prestigious venue for John to meet privately with his most important visitors, such as churchmen and other dignitaries. Entertaining on a grander scale took place in the great hall, a separate two-storey building constructed against the curtain wall near the eastern entrance and with windows looking out over Belfast Lough. This suite of internal buildings also included John's private chapel, a small structure at the north end of the complex.

An important aspect of the life of a great lord was the ostentatious display of his wealth. Social status was indicated by the high quality and fineness of the clothes John and Affreca wore, their gold and jewelled adornments and their well-bred horses. It was impossible to mistake a lord for someone of lower status because he would have literally dazzled the eye with the opulence of his costume and the superior manner in which he acted.

Carrickfergus Castle was an example of the ostentatious display of wealth characteristic of the Norman aristocratic elite from which John was drawn. Its size, strength and location all indicated the wealth of its builder and owner. To own such a castle showed that the lord controlled a large area of land and ruled over thousands of peasants. Staffing the castle, filling the stables with fine stallions, and the quality of the foods being prepared in the kitchen – another separate building inside the curtain wall – all signalled that John was master of a substantial territory. Above all else, Carrickfergus Castle proclaimed that John lived in a truly regal style, that he was Prince of Ulster.

While John's lordship of Ulster can be mapped as the land east of the river Bann, his influence also stretched out into the surrounding seas from his capital at Carrickfergus. John's marriage to Affreca, daughter of the king of the Isle of Man, in 1180, was not just about establishing an important alliance. It linked his lordship to a maritime power influential in a region centred on the northern Irish Sea and meant that John de Courcy's Ulster functioned virtually without hindrance from any king or other great lord.

As a Norman, the king of England was John's nominal overlord, but he acted as if he owed allegiance to no one. The king's pronouncements – or those of the king of Scotland – had little influence over his lordship. To the north, covering the Hebrides, was the all-but-independent lordship of the Isles which, if it owed allegiance to anyone, was nominally part of the territory of the king of Norway. To the north-east of Ulster were the separate earldoms of Carrick and Galloway which were still centuries away from being incorporated into the kingdom of Scotland. Eastwards across the sea was Cumbria, remote from the influence of any king and with plenty of John de Courcy's family connections. Moreover, most of what we now think of as northern England and southern Scotland was claimed by both kingdoms and usually only under the control of its local independently-minded lords. They only gave deference to kings when they were confronted by royal armies. To the south-east of John's lordship were the autonomous principalities of Wales. These remained independent for another century or more until conquered by King Edward I of England.

In Ireland, John's Ulster existed amongst independent Irish kingdoms. These isolated John from the semi-independent Norman lordships in the south and east of Ireland which themselves paid heed to the king of England's officials in Dublin only when forced to do so. Carrickfergus Castle was a statement of John's strength and importance within this milieu of independent territories and it was the focus of his lordship. It all came to an end when he was confronted by King John of England and forcibly stripped of his lordship. Thereafter, Carrickfergus Castle was enlarged and became the centre of royal authority in Ulster until the twentieth century.

Markets were the main way in which John forcibly transformed the indigenous Irish economy into one familiar to the Anglo-Normans. He introduced silver half-pennies and farthings to promote the use of coinage instead of barter exchange, and also to demonstrate just how independent his lordship was from the king of England. His two main mints were at Carrickfergus and Downpatrick, but there may have been others. John also introduced those organisational aspects of lordship which he had learnt as a youth. He made Richard fitz Robert his steward charged with the job of running Ulster's routine administration, and he appointed Roger of Chester as his constable. Roger was responsible for organising John's fighting men and looking after his castles. The medieval office of constable developed from the man put in charge of his lord's horses and stables: he literally had the 'con' (oversight) of the 'stable'. A constable's duties quickly grew in this period until he was responsible for the day-to-day management of one or more castles. It is very likely that Roger was based at Carrickfergus Castle for at least some of these duties.

John's primary method of transforming Irish Ulster into an Anglo-Norman lordship was, however, to make grants of land, dividing his newly-won territory into local manors which could be tenanted by Normans who had accompanied him to Ireland and those in his wide-ranging family connections in Britain who sought land for themselves. These men then established their own Anglo-Norman families in Ulster, controlled and protected the Irish peasantry who continued to make up the local workforce, and created a new social elite in the region.

Patronage

In the twelfth century, the Church was a valuable ally to any lord or king. Abbeys and dioceses owned land and formed part of a vast single international organisation. Making grants to the church allowed John to introduce monks from abbeys associated with the Courcys in England and Normandy, and also helped him to influence the appointment of bishops of the dioceses which covered his lordship or were adjacent. Moreover, moveable wealth, in the form of gold and silver objects, could be donated in good times and then 'recovered' when cash was needed. The monks might complain but no doubt John would have regarded a wooden crucifix as being just as effective as a silver one.

John's patronage was very much a family affair. In about 1179, John revived the defunct monastery of Nendrum, on Strangford Lough, and granted it as a daughter house to the abbey of St Bees in Copeland, within the lordship of his aunt, Alice de Rumilly, widow of William fitz Duncan. St Bees had been founded by William Meschin, Alice's father. Alice was John's aunt by marriage. Later, John established Inch Abbey at Downpatrick for the Cistercians as a daughter house of Furness Abbey. Furness was deep within Alice de Rumilly's lordship of Egremont, just across the Irish Sea.

John's links with Furness were especially strong and he commissioned one of the abbey's monks, Jocelin, to write a new Life of Saint Patrick to help promote the saint's cult at Downpatrick. It is from Jocelin's dedication to John at the beginning of this work that we get his description as princeps – top man, prince – of Ulster.

In 1183, John founded a Benedictine priory at Ards, dependent on Saint Andrew's Priory in Stogursey in Somerset from where its first monks were drawn. This was another clear link with his family as Stogursey was, of course, Stoke Courcy and the centre of his uncle's lordship. At the same time, John founded the cathedral chapter of Downpatrick with Benedictine monks drawn from Saint Werburgh's Abbey in Chester, the principal recipient of the earl of Chester's patronage. The earl was William Meschin's nephew and his family traced its line back to the lords of the Bessin in Normandy, with whom the Courcys had established close ties in the eleventh century. John was paying full homage to his past and strengthening all the complex family links that he enjoyed. A further example of John's family-based patronage was his founding of the priory of Saint Thomas the Martyr for Augustinian canons at Toberglory, in Downpatrick. Toberglory became a dependent house of Saint Mary's Abbey in Carlisle, situated on the northern boundary of the Rumilly lordship, and with links to David, king of Scots, uncle of William fitz Duncan.

John's patronage never strayed far from his family ties. Through his wife, Affreca, he again made the Cistercians his beneficiaries in the early 1190s, founding Grey Abbey, near the head of Strangford Lough, as a daughter house of Holm Cultram Abbey in Cumberland. Tradition has it that Affreca is buried at Grey Abbey but unfortunately the stone effigy attributed to her dates from the fourteenth century rather than the first half of the thirteenth century. Grey Abbey's proper name is Iugum Dei, the Yoke of God. The story goes that Affreca founded the abbey in praise of God for answering her prayers during a stormy sea voyage, presumably to or from Man. It could well be true but its establishment was also part of her husband's strategy of tying the church into his lordship. Apart from the still-extant ruins of its buildings, stone fish traps have been discovered nearby on the foreshore of Strangford Lough. It also owned a lucrative sea fishery at Ballywalter on the eastern coast of the Ards peninsula.

John's final act of patronage, according to the surviving evidence, was the creation of a house for Premonstratensian canons at Carrickfergus with monks drawn from Dryburgh Abbey in Berwickshire. Dryburgh had been founded by the Morville family and was patronised by the kings of Scotland so, by making this donation, John was signalling his links via William fitz Duncan with the Scottish crown and his friendship with families based in north-west

England and south-west Scotland. In this way he tried to limit the influence of the king of England over his lordship of Ulster by playing him off against the king of Scotland.

Tenants

We can discover the names of some of John's aristocratic tenants from the witness lists on surviving charters of the time. These charters granted land or other benefits to religious organisations, such as the monastic houses he founded. Charters were issued to secular individuals as well, such as tenants, but almost invariably the ones that survive relate to religious houses, so the evidence for John's grants is limited. This is because religious houses insisted on receiving a written statement of any grant and carefully preserved such documentation. Also, the act of granting a charter was made verbally, perhaps with an action such as placing a dagger on an altar, and the written charter was a record of that act, not the act itself. This seems strange in our modern society with its obsession for written records, but in medieval society it was verbal statements which carried weight. Secular recipients either did not receive written charters or, most often, did not give them value after the death of the lord making the grant.

Looking at the surviving charters issued by John de Courcy, once we eliminate nicknames and isolated first names, we have about 30 individuals who can be associated with a place of origin. Unsurprisingly, almost all of these came from northern England but a few can be linked to Courcy estates elsewhere. For example, John's steward, Richard fitz Robert, is probably a son of a leading Courcy tenant in Northamptonshire. Roger of Chester, John's constable, was almost certainly one of the earl of Chester's men. He held a manor at Crumlin, near Lough Neagh. We know this because John of Chester, Roger's son, subsequently made a grant of tithes from his lands all round Lough Neagh to the Hospital of Saint John the Baptist in Dublin. Despite his father's name, John of Chester later called himself John de Courcy when, in 1204, he was one of several hostages taken by King John.

This name change, along with references to a Milo 'son of John de Courcy' and, subsequently a Patrick de Courcy in the royal records, suggest that the lord of Ulster may have produced several sons with women other than his wife. The genealogy of the de Courcy lords of Kinsale relies on this last supposed son of John but there is no evidence that he had any children. It is likely that the name was used to identify men of his retinue, those 'of Courcy', and Milo may just be a transliteration of miles, a soldier, of Courcy.

Other tenants drawn from Chester include Richard Fitton, who commanded Mount Sandel Castle in 1197, and Elias of Chester, based at Ballymoran, near Killinchy, on the western shores of Strangford Lough. Elias was a patron of Nendrum Abbey, just up the coast, and also held the motte-and-bailey castle at Rathgorman which overlooked Quarterland Bay and controlled the natural harbour of Ringhaddy. Elias also made a grant to a Dublin religious house from land held in the district and this may mean he was one of the original garrison group which accompanied John northwards.

Apart from those from Chester, the names of John's tenants indicate a wide sweep of territory: Gilbert of Furness, Gilbert and Roger de Croft (Warrington), Robert Vardcap (Warcop near Appleby), and Richard son of Truite (linked with eastern Cumberland and Galloway). Jocelin de Cailly was the son of a tenant of Cecily de Rumilly and two others were identified as 'of Copeland', showing their origins in the Cumbrian lordship. William and Henry Copland gave their name to the townland of Ballycopeland in the Ards, and the Copeland Islands, just off the coast. The name Copeland also occurs near Carrickfergus, but it was probably the motte at Donaghadee, overlooking the harbour and now surmounted by a Victorian dynamite store, which formed the centre of the manors they tenanted from John.

From Yorkshire, John granted Augustine de Ridale (Ryedale, North Riding) the area around Ballyeaston in County Antrim. Roger de Dunesforthe (Dunsforth, West Riding) gave his name to Dunsfort and was given land north of Ardglass, County Down by John. Yorkshire also provided Brian de Scaliers (Pontefract, West Riding) as the tenant of Ballydargan, further west round the coast and a little inland on the road to Clough. Other probable Yorkshire tenants were the families of Sandall, Talbot, Hacket and Maitland.

Similarly, John gained tenant settlers from south-east Scotland, especially Galloway and around the Solway Firth. This was another area which he knew well from wide-ranging visits to local lords during his adolescence. Finally, John's marriage to Affreca, the daughter of the king of Man, added a new network of alliances which spanned the Irish Sea uniting political entities which regarded themselves as independent, or nearly so, of the unitary kingdoms of England and Scotland and the influence of their kings.

John's campaigns

It is difficult to uncover John's history after his success at Downpatrick for the only records are the very terse and occasionally ambiguous entries in the Irish annals, and a handful of references in the administrative rolls of the kings of England. The latter only appear when he comes into conflict with the wily King John. Nevertheless, according to the Annals of Tigonach, the house chronicle of the Connacht royal dynasty, John de Courcy was defeated by the Irish soon after his second victory at Downpatrick and briefly taken prisoner. This may have been at the hands of Rory O'Connor, who claimed to be overlord of Ulaid. In the following year, 1178, John was defeated twice in battle when campaigning first towards Coleraine and then southwards into Louth. It may have been these defeats that prompted his building of Carrickfergus Castle to strengthen his position.

He had stabilised things by the following year and began negotiations with the king of Man. These culminated in 1180 with John's marriage to Affreca, the daughter of King Godred of Man. Apart from the link she brought with the ruling family of Man, Affreca was also connected to the Lords of the Isles (ie the Hebrides). Moreover, she was a niece of Somerled, the powerful and charismatic lord of Argyll and the Isles. John himself was also related in some way now undetermined to Duncan, earl of Carrick in Galloway, and he subsequently granted his Galwegian cousin lands near Coleraine in 1197. Consequently, it may be claimed that Duncan's settlers were the first Ulster Scots. Aided by his Manx connection, John built up a small fleet of ships, based at Coleraine. He subsequently won control of land west of the Bann estuary in the later 1180s and it was here that he planted further Scottish settlers. John's lordship was always under threat, particularly from the MacLoughlins. In 1181, Donal MacLoughlin invaded but was defeated, while in 1183 Malachy MacLoughlin was murdered by some of John's men.

John may have visited King Henry II in England about then and it has been suggested that at their meeting he was appointed the king's justiciar of Ireland, although it is extremely unlikely. John did supervise the Lacy honour in Meath on the king's behalf after its lord was killed by Gilla-gan-inathair O Mee but this was far short of a justiciarship. In 1185, Prince John, the brother of King Richard of England, was made lord of Ireland and formally accepted John de Courcy's homage. This was the first stage in the royal government's plan to bring the independently-minded lord of Ulster under its control.

John de Courcy faced hostile Irish lordships along the length of the river Bann, but true to his nature his main means of defence was attack. In 1188, part of John's army marched across Armagh towards Dungannon, but was beaten back by Donal MacLoughlin. At the same time John led an Anglo-Norman force towards Connacht, but turned north towards Ballysadare and Donegal. They had probably been hired as mercenaries by Rory O'Connor to help him regain his lordship of Connacht and oust his usurping son Conchobar. John met stiff opposition and was forced to retreat across the Curlew Mountains. He then changed course, but was attacked by the Irish of Connacht and suffered heavy losses, forcing him to retreat.

In 1189, Prince John appointed his own men, Bertram de Verdun and Gilbert Pipard, to hold Dundalk and Ardee respectively. This new royal Anglo-Norman presence stretched towards the southern border of John de Courcy's lordship and began the feudalisation and settlement of previously independent Irish areas separating Ulster from the English king's territories around Dublin. John responded with a show of force, marching on Armagh and then waging a large-scale raid into Fermanagh.

John de Courcy reached the zenith of his power in 1194 when King Richard the Lionheart finally made him royal justiciar of Ireland. However, just as Fortune's wheel had spun John to the very pinnacle of achievement it was also preparing to bring him down.

Cathal Crobderg, ruler of Connacht, invaded Thomond in 1195 and, to protect his rear, agreed a peace treaty at Athlone with John de Courcy and Walter de Lacy. Cathal mustered more than twelve hundred men while, according to the Annals of Loch Cé, John de Courcy and Walter de Lacy assumed the leadership of the Anglo-Normans of Leinster and Munster. The treaty also secured John de Courcy's flank as he capitalised on the situation by joining with local Irish lords, including Rory MacDunlevy, in co-ordinated attacks to attempt to capture territory west of the Bann. Dunlevy attacked the O'Neills, but was defeated. John fortified Mount Sandel near Coleraine and campaigned in the region between

Toomebridge and Derry. Simultaneously he launched attacks with his fleet along the north coast, but the raid, led by one of his lieutenants, was not a success and was beaten off by the inhabitants. Soon after, a separate sea-borne raid on the Inishowen met with a similar fate and failed.

John was again campaigning in 1197, travelling across Tyrone to Ardstraw and Derry. He ravaged the Inishowen, but faced stiff opposition from the now united O'Neills. In an attempt to relieve the pressure on their western territories, Aedh O'Neill of Tyrone attacked the east of John's lordship. He made a landing near Larne with five ships and overran Kilwaughter before withdrawing. It is perhaps significant that he didn't contemplate attacking John's castle at Carrickferrgus. John retreated from the Inishowen but, according to the Irish chronicles, he took with him many cattle, this perhaps being one of his chief objectives. He returned to the attack against the O'Neills two years later, launching three separate campaigns, or hostings as they were known, into Tyrone. In the last of these he was finally brought to battle and beaten by Aedh O'Neill near Donaghmore.

By 1200 Cathal Crobderg of Connacht was again resurgent and now had the support of Aedh O'Neill and John de Courcy. Together, the forces of O'Neill and de Courcy moved into north Connacht, pillaging Roscommon and Sligo on the way. They were ranged against Cathal Carrach, the nephew of Cathal Cobderg, who sought to replace his uncle in Connacht and who enjoyed the support of William de Burgo, the leading Norman colonist in Tipperary, who could also muster an Anglo-Norman army. O'Neill withdrew his native forces, being harried by Cathal Carrach, and was driven back as far as Drumcliff. John de Courcy and Hugh de Lacy, however, rallied their men and moved towards Kilmacduagh before confronting Cathal Carrach at Tuam. They were defeated and withdrew eastwards with some difficulty, being ferried across Lough Ree.

The end

For John, however, the days of the free-ranging campaigning which he enjoyed so much were drawing to a close, largely as a result of the patchwork and disjointed colonisation and settlement of Ireland by the Anglo-Normans themselves. John de Courcy's freebooting activities provided a convenient reason for increased royal involvement in Ireland. King Richard had died and his younger brother, the erstwhile lord of Ireland, was now King John of England and his sights were set on the lord of Ulster. John de Courcy's independent attitude was the king's target.

In 1202, King John invited the lord of Ulster to travel to England under safe conduct in order to make peace. John de Courcy wisely declined the offer. By the following year relations between the two had deteriorated even further. King John was less than impressed that de Courcy was minting coins which bore the name of Saint Patrick rather than that of the king. John belatedly complied, but the affront still rankled. Walter de Lacy was authorised by the king to seize John de Courcy and imprison him at Nobber in County Louth. John was popular amongst his fellow Anglo-Norman lords, however, and when his Ulster tenants and Irish allies mustered at Nobber in his support, Walter de Lacy pragmatically released him. John's tenants attempted to defuse the king's rapidly escalating hostility by offering their sons as hostages, but were refused. Instead, King John instructed the Lacy lords to invade and seize Ulster. It was perhaps no coincidence that this family was selected as it was they who had suffered at the hands of William fitz Duncan many years before at the Battle of Clitheroe. John de Courcy counted William fitz Duncan, lord of Skipton, as his relation.

The last act in the story of John de Courcy began in 1204, when King John ordered the construction of Dublin Castle as the seat of royal government. This showed that the king of England was now going to exercise his personal authority over Anglo-Norman Ireland. John de Courcy had returned to Ulster from Nobber, but now faced the Lacy invasion. Hugh de Lacy captured John, seized his lordship and dispossessed him of all he had.

John pledged to take the cross and go on crusade. He convinced Hugh of his sincerity and was released. This move was subsequently copied by King John of England during his fight against his barons, which ultimately led to the signing of Magna Carta. By taking the cross a Norman lord's family and property were given the protection of the Church. In Ireland, John de Courcy's action probably suited Hugh's purpose because if John tried to recapture his lordship, rather than heading for Jerusalem, he would have broken his oath and his complete dispossession could be sanctioned by the king acting on the Church's behalf.

Once again, John gambled on the situation and decided not to go on crusade. He rallied support from his kinsmen, allies and neighbouring native Irish lords. The most valuable help came from his brother-in-law, the king of Man, who supplied a fleet of ships. King John reacted on 29 May 1205. John de Courcy was formally stripped of his land in Ireland and it was all granted to Hugh de Lacy who was then invested with the new title and honour of earl of Ulster. John, meanwhile, arrived at Strangford with his fleet of ships and supporters, and moved swiftly round the coast to besiege Hugh at Dundrum Castle. Hugh's brother, Walter de Lacy, rushed northwards with an army to support his brother. John de Courcy's siege was unsuccessful and his forces were defeated.

Just what happened next is unclear. One story says that John retired to his English manors. However,

Middleton and his other Northamptonshire lands were being administered by the husband of Alice de Courcy of Stogursey, the surviving heiress of the English de Courcy line. Also, King John was notoriously vindictive and it is unlikely that he would have allowed John de Courcy to simply 'spend more time with his family'. At the very least he would have imprisoned John in a royal castle, as he did with various lords and their families who displeased him.

A more plausible story is that John de Courcy fled to France, to his family's lands in Normandy. It was at about this time that the duchy was captured by the king of France and Robert de Courcy, lord of Courcy-sur-Dives, was on the ascendant. Robert quickly became an important figure in the new royal administration controlling the duchy. Normandy lost its independence as part of the land of the king of England and became just another province of the kingdom of France. John de Courcy sought sanctuary from his distant cousin and spent the next two years keeping his head down. In 1207, with the king of England's permission, John returned to the country of his birth and was reconciled with his sovereign. He settled at Middleton and had no further involvement in Ulster.

Or at least that's how that particular version of his last years has it. There is some evidence to suggest that John's specialist knowledge of Ireland was used by the king for his expedition in 1210 and, six years later, that he was sent to command troops at Winchester to defend the city against the invading force of Louis of France. Another version has it that after this service John retired to a monastery in Chester to live out his final years. This was a conventional way for a dying lord to spend his last months and John certainly had family links with the earldom. A further anecdote places John's last days in a French monastery.

We don't know when or where John died, but the royal records of England show that he was deceased by 1219. In that year, Affreca's possession of her widow's dower lands was confirmed by the king. This dower land had been made over to her by her husband John as part of their marriage agreement, in order to support her should he die before her. These particular manors lay west of the river Bann and included land over which the O'Neills had disputed ownership with John de Courcy for some considerable time. John could have died some years earlier.

Yet the stories continued. Another legend has John fighting a duel as the champion of the boy-king Henry III. For this fanciful tale, set in the 1220s, John would have been in his 70s, although his great age and well-documented fighting ability are key elements of the scene described. While far-fetched, it sums up his contemporaries' image of this charismatic warrior who posed such a contrast to Henry III's scheming, unpopular and unsuccessful father, King John.

John de Courcy personified the idealised self-image of the Anglo-Norman knight. He conquered new territory, he was courageous, he led his men from the front and was always in the thick of the action, just like William the Conqueror. In an age of division, destruction and loss, John de Courcy symbolised the ideal Anglo-Norman warrior lord to his fellow aristocrats. His destruction at the hands of the devious and villainous King John adds extra poignancy to his story. As the dawn mists slowly cleared over Downpatrick they revealed a true Norman hero on his white horse, his army ranged behind him, ready for conquest. John stepped into history as the prophetically-foretold star of his own wild romance and, at its end, he disappeared back into the realms of adventure, tale-telling and legend.

Maps

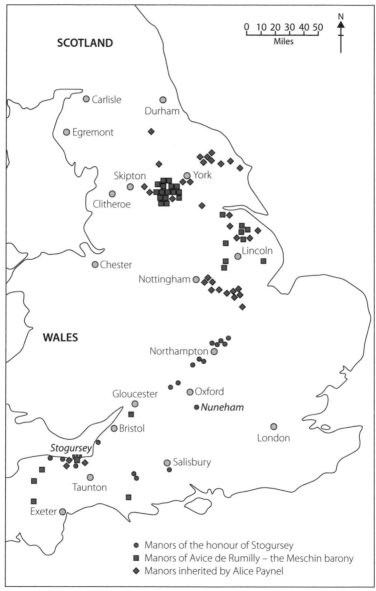

Map 1: Manors held by the Courcy family in England in about 1135.

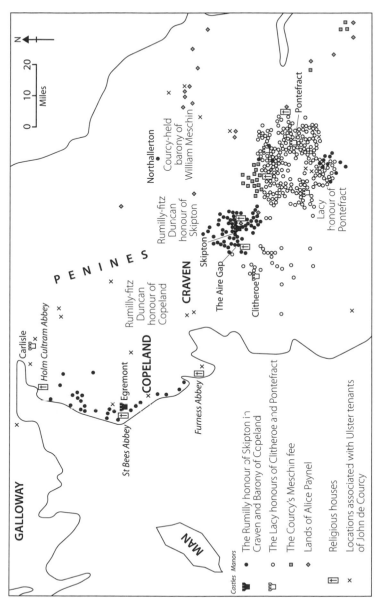

Map 2: Northern England and Galloway in the twelfth century showing the manors and castles held by the Courcy, fitz Duncan and Lacy families.

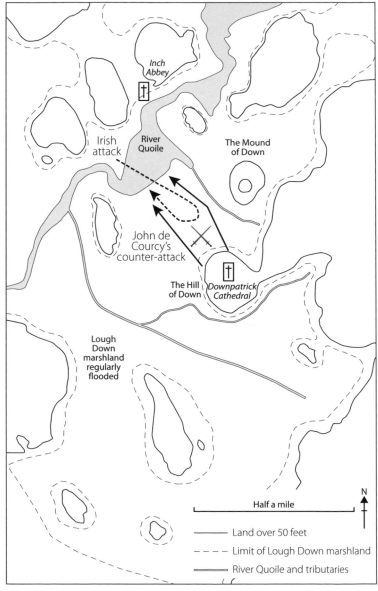

Map 3: The battle site at Downpatrick.

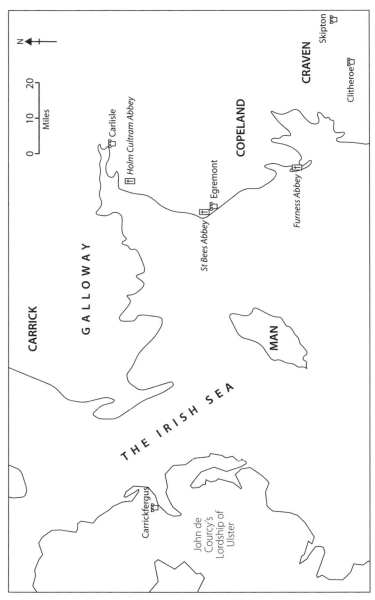

Map 4: The Irish Sea provided John de Courcy with an excellent transport network that linked him to many other independent lordships.

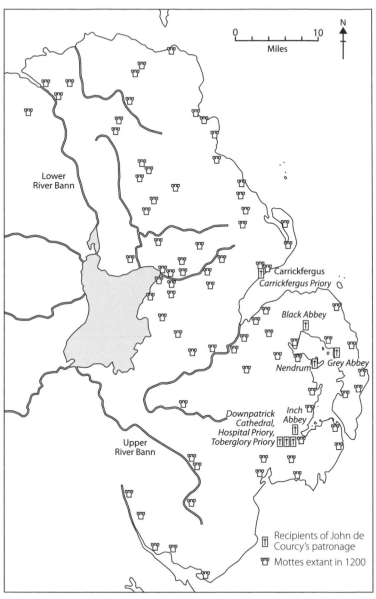

Map 5: John de Courcy's lordship.

Figures

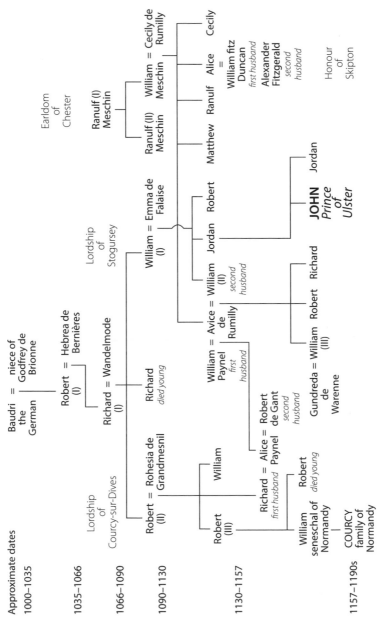

Figure 1: The Courcy family in the eleventh and twelfth centuries.

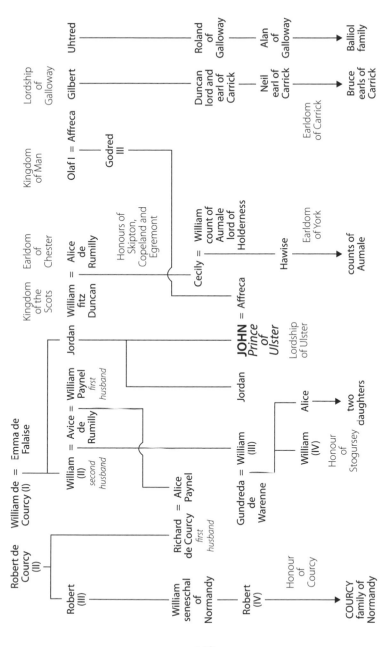

Figure 2: The lordships with which John de Courcy could claim a close family relationship.

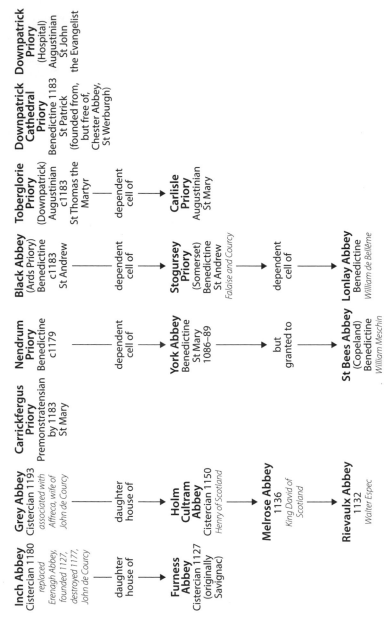

Figure 3: John de Courcy's religious patronage: foundations, refoundations and grants.

Index